MONTRÉAL & QUÉBEC CITY

TOP EXPERIENCES • LOCAL LIFE

REGIS ST LOUIS, STEVE FALLON,
PHILLIP TANG, JOHN LEE

Contents

Plan Your Trip 4

Stained-glass window, Basilique Notre-Dame (p30), Montréal BENEDEK/GETTY IMAGES ©

Explore Montréal 27

Explore Québec City 113

Survival Guide 145

COVID-19

We have re-checked every business in this book before publication to ensure that it is still open after the COVID-19 outbreak. However, the economic and social impacts of COVID-19 will continue to be felt long after the outbreak has been contained, and many businesses, services and events referenced in this guide may experience ongoing restrictions. Some may be temporarily closed, have changed their opening hours and services, or require bookings; some unfortunately could have closed permanently. We suggest you check with venues before visiting for the latest information.

Special Features

Top Experiences

MEUNIERD/SHUTTERSTOCK ©

Visit Canada's oldest museum: Musée des Beaux-Arts de Montréal (p52)

Take in the views from Oratoire St-Joseph, Montréal (p110)

Attend the Aura Basilica at Basilique Notre-Dame, Montréal (p30)

DENIS ROGER/SHUTTERSTOCK ©

Learn about the people of Québec at the Musée de la Civilisation, Québec City (p120)

CL-MEDIEN/SHUTTERSTOCK © ARCHITECT, MOSHE SAFDIE

Watch the world go by on Rue St-Denis, Montréal (p68)

Stroll through the leafy islands of Parc Jean-Drapeau, Montréal (p46)

Discover Québec's military history at La Citadelle, Québec City (p116)

Grab a fancy seat at Le Château Frontenac's bar or bistro, Québec City (p118)

Dining Out

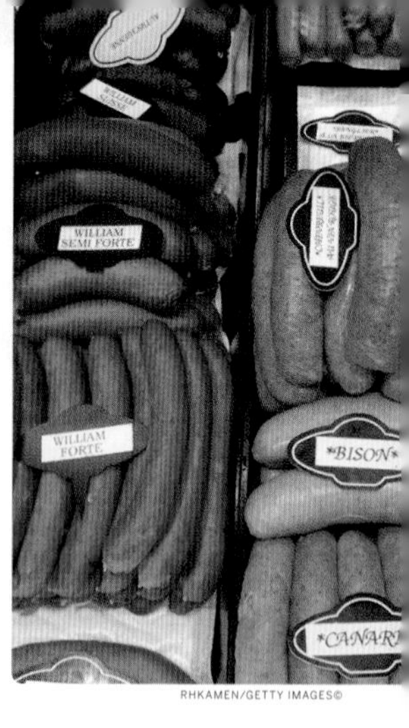

RHKAMEN/GETTY IMAGES©

Montréal and Québec City are foodie destinations. You'll find French cuisine, charming bistros and Québécois fare. Montréal's many restaurants have cuisine from over 80 nationalities. Today's haute cuisine is as likely to be made by talented young African, Japanese or Indian chefs, as it is by graduates from the Académie Culinaire du Québec.

Poutine

One of the world's most humble dishes, poutine (pictured above right) was invented in rural Québec in the 1950s ('poutine' derives from an Acadian slang term for 'mushy mess' or 'pudding.'). The basic building block of the Québécois dish is fries smothered in cheese curds and gravy. Varieties include 'all dress' (sautéed mushrooms and bell peppers), 'richie boy' (ground beef), Italian (beef and spaghetti sauce), barbecue or even smoked meat.

Markets

For a slice of old-world Europe, don't miss Montréal's sprawling food markets. You'll find a broad selection of fruits, vegetables, fresh bakery items, cheeses and more. The big markets have plenty of stands selling prepared foods (crepes, smoothies, coffees, pastries, sandwiches, pizza slices and more).

The biggest Montréal market is **Marché Jean-Talon** (p94) in Little Italy. Runner-up **Marché Atwater** (p105), just west of downtown near the Canal de Lachine, is a fine spot for a picnic. In Québec City, **Les Halles Cartier** (p141) has enticing offerings.

Best Eating in Montréal

Garde-Manger Celebrated Old Montréal haunt with a festive vibe. (p40)

Joe Beef Creative meats and seafood, excellent wines and knowledgeable staff. (p108)

Au Pied de Cochon Beautifully executed dishes, including foie gras poutine. (p83)

Barroco Stone walls, flickering candles, great cocktails and market-fresh fare. (p40)

P.F.MAYER/SHUTTERSTOCK ©

Olive + Gourmando Delicious baked goods and outstanding lunch fare. (p39)

Best Eating in Québec City

Chez Boulay Chef Jean-Luc Boulay's flagship restaurant serves an ever-evolving menu inspired by seasonal Québécois staples. (p129)

Buvette Scott Tiny wine bistro in trendy St-Jean Baptiste serving enlightened French classics. (p141)

Le Lapin Sauté *Lapin* (rabbit) in all its guises plays a starring role at this cozy, rustic restaurant. (p128)

Le St-Amour One of Québec City's top fine-dining spots, with prepared grills and seafood and luxurious surrounds. (p130)

Best Global & Ethnic Cuisine in Montréal

Tapas 24 The city's best tapas, from Catalan star Carles Abellán. (p41)

Schwartz's Long-running Jewish deli serving the best smoked meat (pictured above left) on earth. (p81)

Impasto Beloved outpost for fantastic Italian cooking. (p96)

Satay Brothers Asian street food and fusion in a colorful setting. (p106)

Kazu Ramen noodles and Japanese comfort food. (p106)

L'Express Captivating Parisian-style bistro. (p82)

Best Québécois Fare in Québec City

Légende Seasonal cuisine and fine-wine pairings are the name of the game at this very classy eatery. (p129)

Poutineville Unpretentious eatery in St-Roch serving mostly (but not only) poutine, Québec's national dish. (p140)

Bar Open

In Montréal it's acceptable, even expected, to begin cocktail hour after work and continue into the night. The nightlife is legendary: encompassing underground dance clubs, French hip-hop, dub reggae and Anglo indie-rock. Québec City has plenty to offer, including craft breweries, downstairs music clubs and atmospheric wine bars.

ALLEKO/GETTY IMAGES ©

Bars

Montréalers and Québecers treat their bars like a second home, unwinding after work for the legendary *cinq à sept* (5pm to 7pm) happy hour on Thursdays and Fridays, quaffing wine, beer and cocktails; the 7pm cutoff oftens extends until the wee hours. In late spring and summer this is often done on a rooftop patio as temperatures rise. Come winter, locals are undaunted by snowstorms and long, frigid nights. In fact, that's the best time to find a warm, cozy bar (preferably with a roaring fire) and while the night away among friends and a few creative libations.

What's On

For club, bar and other entertainment listings in Montréal, check out www.nightlife.ca and MTL Blog (www.mtlblog.com). In Québec City, pick up the monthly **Quoi Faire à Québec** (www.quoifaireaquebec.com), available at bars, clubs, restaurants and tourist offices everywhere. **Voir Québec** (https://voir.ca) is a good French-language entertainment and listings website.

Best Nightlife in Montréal

Le Mal Necessaire Tasty libations stirred up in a hidden Chinatown drinking den. (p43)

Big in Japan Magical setting for a fancy drink. (p83)

Best Nightlife in Québec City

Griendel Brasserie Artisanale At this St-Sauveur boozer, you can choose from two dozen *broues* (brews), most of which are brewed in house. (p141)

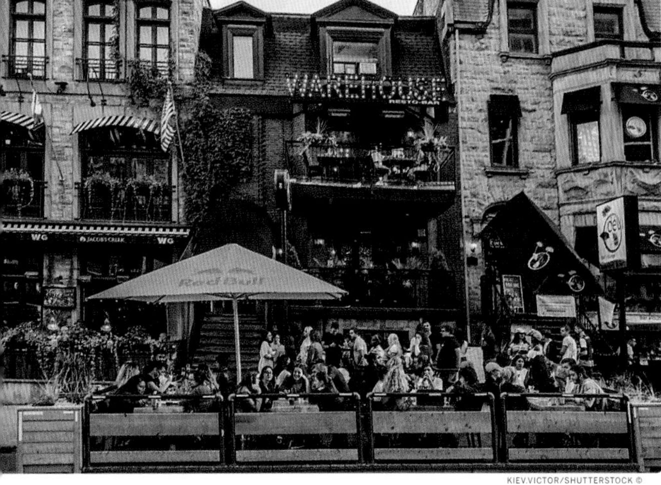

KIEV.VICTOR/SHUTTERSTOCK ©

Bar Ste-Angèle Low-lit, intimate hipster hangout in the Old Town, with occasional live jazz sessions. (p130)

Le Sacrilège Excellent brews, great atmosphere and an appealing terrace on clear nights. (p142)

L'Oncle Antoine Great tavern in a vaulted brick cellar pouring excellent Québec microbrews on draft. (p128)

Best for Wine

Pullman Extensive wine list and buzzing early-evening gathering spot in downtown Montréal. (p63)

Le Vin Papillon Much lauded wine-focused eatery in Montréal's Little Burgundy district. (p106)

Le Moine Échanson Convivial brick-walled Québec City wine bar pouring an ever-changing array of vintages from all over the Mediterranean. (p142)

Best Brewpubs

Isle de Garde A Montréal gem in Little Italy with great beer and a friendly crowd. (p97)

Les Sœurs Grises A classy brasserie in Old Montréal. (p43)

Brutopia Buzzing brew pub with live music nightly in downtown Montréal. (p64)

Noctem Artisans Brasseurs This Québec City place has a blackboard of up to 18 different beers and ales that change daily. (p141)

Best Cafes

Crew Café Sumptuous converted bank for bagels and laptop time in Old Montréal. (p42)

Chez Temporel Charming little cafe on an Old Town (Québec City) side street serving fresh baked goods and excellent coffee. (p127)

Showtime

The performing arts flourish in Montréal and Québec City. Live performance venues abound, from concert halls to open-air amphitheaters, jazz and rock clubs, and boîtes à chanson (Québec folk-music clubs). Montréal's bilingualism makes it creatively unique and encourages collaborations and cross-pollinations that light up the scene.

Live Music

Montréal is a music powerhouse, fostering an incredible variety of talent from cabaret pop stars such as Patrick Watson to rock stars like Leonard Cohen; jazz legends such as Oscar Peterson; and ex–Mile End resident, electro-pop artist Grimes. Catch rising stars of the underground and indie music community in artsy Plateau venues such as Casa del Popolo. Major acts from elsewhere perform at bigger venues like the Bell Centre. In Québec City, a number of bars and clubs host regular live-music performances, especially in St-Jean Baptiste and St-Roch.

Dance

Considered Canada's dance capital, Montréal boasts an avant-garde and vibrant dance scene. Styles such as ballet, modern, jazz, hip-hop, Latin social dancing and tango exist side by side with contemporary dance that fuses various styles and incorporates theater, music and digital art.

Best Performing Arts

Place des Arts (Map p56, F3; ☎box office 514-842-2112; www.placedesarts.com; 175 Rue Ste-Catherine Ouest; M Place-des-Arts) Performing-arts complex (pictured), home to everything from jazz to ballet and opera.

Grand Théâtre de Québec (Map p136, D5; ☎877-643-8131, 418-643-8131; www.grandtheatre.qc.ca; 269 Blvd René-Lévesque Est, Montcalm & Colline Parlementaire; ⌚box office noon-5pm Mon-Sat & 30min before performances) Québec City's main performing arts center with top-quality classical concerts, opera, dance and theater.

JEFFREY ISAAC GREENBERG 2+/ALAMY STOCK PHOTO ©

Gesú (Map p56, F4; ☎514-861-4378; www.legesu.com; 1200 Rue de Bleury; shows $18-57; ⏰box office noon-6:30pm Tue-Sat) Intimate church-basement venue in downtown Montréal with a wide-ranging repertoire.

Best Live Music in Montréal

Dièse Onze (Map p78, E4; ☎514-223-3543; www.dieseonze.com; 4115 Rue St-Denis; $10; ⏰6pm-late; Ⓜ Mont-Royal) Atmospheric basement jazz den in the Plateau.

Casa del Popolo (Map p78, C1; ☎514-284-0122; www.casadelpopolo.com; 4873 Blvd St-Laurent; $5-20; ⏰noon-3am; Ⓜ Laurier) One of the best indie-music venues in the city.

Best Live Music in Québec City

Bar Les Yeux Bleus (Map p124, B3; ☎418-694-9118; 1117 Rue St-Jean, Old Upper Town; ⏰9pm-3am Mon, Tue & Thu, 8pm-3am Wed, 4pm-3am Fri-Sun, closed Mon-Wed winter) This boîte à chanson (folk-music club) is the place to catch newcomers and Québécois classics.

Pape Georges (Map p124, E4; ☎418-692-1320; https://facebook.com/papegeorges; 8 Rue de Cul-de-Sac, Old Lower Town & Port; ⏰11am-3pm) This charming bar in a 400-year-old house has music on Friday and Saturday nights (more in summer).

Best Theaters

Centaur Theatre (Map p44, C4; ☎514-288-3161; www.centaurtheatre.com; 453 Rue St-François-Xavier; Ⓜ Place-d'Armes) Top English-language performances in a memorable Old Montréal locale.

Monument National (Map p56, G4; ☎514-871-2224; www.monumentnational.com; 1182 Blvd St-Laurent; Ⓜ St-Laurent) Showcases theater, dance and comedy in a grand 19th-century building in downtown Montréal.

Le Théâtre Capitole (☎800-261-9903, 418-694-4444; www.lecapitole.com; 972 Rue St-Jean, St-Jean Baptiste) Historic theater hosting cabaret and musical revues in Québec City.

Treasure Hunt

S. GREG PANOSIAN/GETTY IMAGES ©

Montréal is an ideal shopping city which offers everything from big international department stores to high-fashion designers, vintage clothing boutiques to weird one-of-a-kind antique shops, used-music stores and booksellers, chic home decor and more. Québec City is best known for its unique and authentic boutiques.

Best Shopping in Montréal

Eva B Step into an alternate universe in downtown Montréal's wild vintage emporium. (p65)

Drawn & Quarterly A fine collection of literary works and graphic novels, including its own imprint. (p99)

Artpop Eye-catching T-shirts, bags and frame-worthy prints of Montréal landmarks. (p85)

Espace Pepin Artful housewares and fashion pieces in Old Montréal. (p45)

Best Shopping in Québec City

Galerie d'Art Inuit Brousseau Pricey but stunning Inuit soapstone and basalt carvings and sculptures from artists all over Arctic Canada. (p131)

Artisans Canada Superb emporium crammed with Canadian-only arts and crafts, clothing, jewelry and quality souvenirs. (p131)

JA Moisan Épicier North America's oldest grocery is packed with beautifully displayed edibles and kitchen and household items. (p135)

Boutique Métiers d'Art du Québec This stylish boutique stocks Québécois porcelain, ceramics, jewelry, woodcarving and many unusual gifts. (p131)

Best Markets

Marché Jean-Talon Montréal's biggest and best food market (pictured) is in Little Italy. (p94)

Marché Atwater The second-largest produce market in Montréal stands near the Canal de Lachine west of downtown. (p105)

Museums & Galleries

THE MONTRÉAL MUSEUM OF FINE ARTS, JEAN-NOËL DESMARAIS PAVILION. BENOIT DAOUST/SHUTTERSTOCK ©

Montréal has a thriving arts scene, and its galleries offer everything from old masters to works by contemporary artists. Québec City's museums chart the military and cultural history of Canada's French-speaking province.

Best Public Art

Fresque des Québécois Multistory trompe-l'oeil mural of Samuel de Champlain, Jacques Cartier and other Québécois notables. (p123)

Illuminated Crowd This sidewalk sculpture in downtown Montréal offers a rather dark view of humanity. (p55)

Best Art Museums & Galleries in Montréal

Musée des Beaux-Arts de Montréal Old masters and contemporary artists. (pictured; p52)

Musée d'Art Contemporain A weighty collection of artworks from Québécois legends. (p58)

Fonderie Darling Cutting-edge installations in a hidden corner of Old Montréal. (p37)

Best History Museums in Montréal

Pointe-à-Callière Cité d'Archéologie et d'Histoire de Montréal An excellent history museum built on the spot where European settlers put up their first camp. (p36)

Musée Stewart This old British garrison displays relics from Canada's past. (p47)

Musée Redpath Fascinating natural history collection as well as cultural artifacts from around the globe. (p59)

Best Art Museums & Galleries in Québec City

Musée National des Beaux-Arts du Québec Fabulous repository of historical and contemporary art with go-to restaurant and excellent bookshop. (p138)

Galerie d'Art Inuit Brousseau Finest showroom of Inuit art in town. (p131)

Best History Museums in Québec City

Musée des Plaines d'Abraham Multimedia exhibits immerse visitors in the pivotal battles that shaped Québec's destiny. (p151)

Musée de la Civilisation The only museum in town that regularly focuses on contemporary Québécois issues and culture. (p120)

Musée des Ursulines The story of the teaching Ursuline nuns and their influence in the 17th and 18th centuries. (p126)

Active Montréal & Québec City

Whether it's summer or deepest, darkest winter, you can expect to find Montréal and Québec City locals enjoying life outdoors. Inside the city limits there are picturesque parks and paths ideal for an early morning jog or bike ride, as well as a host of winter sports – skating, cross-country skiing and tobogganing – when the weather turns cold.

MARC BRUXELLE/SHUTTERSTOCK ©

Best Montréal Activities

Parc de La Rivière-des-Mille-Îles (☎450-622-1020; www.parc-mille-iles.qc.ca; 345 Blvd Ste-Rose; kayak/canoe per hour $12.50/13.50, per day $42/44; ⏲9am-6pm, to 8pm Fri & Sat mid-Jun–mid-Aug; M Cartier then bus 73) The Rivière des Mille-Îles near Laval is a great spot for canoeing and kayaking.

Parc des Rapides (☎514-367-1000; cnr Blvd LaSalle & 7e Ave; 🚌58, M De l'Église) This park overlooking the Lachine Rapids attracts hikers, anglers, and cyclists.

La Patinoire Natrel du Vieux Port (Parc du Bassin Bonsecours; adult/child $6/4, skate rental $7; ⏲10am-9pm Mon-Wed, to 10pm Thu-Sun; 🚌14, M Champ-de-Mars) Ice skating at the Old Port (pictured) is quintessentially Montréal. DJs add to the festivities. At Christmas time there's a big nativity scene.

Best Québec City Activities

Glissade de la Terrasse (Terrace Slide; ☎418-528-1884; www.au1884.ca; Terrasse Dufferin, Old Upper Town; per person 1/4 slides $3/10; ⏲10am-5pm Sun-Thu, to 6pm Fri & Sat mid-Dec–mid-Mar; 👪) Invigoratingly fast, triple-chute toboggan open all winter.

Anneau de Glace des Plaines d'Abraham (Plains of Abraham Ice Rink; ☎581-777-0700, 418-691-6733; www.ccbn-nbc.gc.ca/en/activities/plains-abraham-skating-rink; 255 Grande Allée Ouest, Plains of Abraham; skating free, skate rental per 2hr $9.25; ⏲10am-10pm late Dec–mid-Mar; 👪).

Patinoire de la Place d'Youville (Place d'Youville Skating Rink; ☎418-641-6256; www.quebec-cite.com/en/businesses/patinoire-de-la-place-dyouville; 995 Place d'Youville, St-Jean Baptiste; skating free, skate rental $9.25; ⏲noon-10pm Mon-Thu, 10am-10pm Fri-Sun mid-Nov–mid-Mar; 👪) Ice skating at the Old Port is quintessentially Montréal.

Corridor du Littoral & Promenade Samuel-de-Champlain (👪) A 48km recreational running/cycling path along the St Lawrence.

For Kids

ALADIN66/GETTY IMAGES ©

Montréal has many sights for young visitors. Aside from boating in summer and ice skating in winter, neighborhood parks are great places for picnics. In Québec City's Old Town, kids love the street performers and guides in period costume. A slow tour of the Old Town in a calèche (horse-drawn carriage) appeals to the whole family.

Best Outdoor Adventures

Canal de Lachine Go for a spin along the peaceful waterway from Old Montréal out to the Lac St-Louis. (p102)

Plage Jean-Doré Summer swimming and kayaking at the artificial beach on a Parc Jean-Drapeau island. (p48)

La Citadelle In summer, catch the changing of the guard at 10am daily and the drum-pounding beating of the retreat (6pm Saturday). (p116)

La Ronde At Québec's largest amusement park, La Ronde (pictured), kids will experience chills and thrills galore – plus fireworks on some summer nights. (p48)

Parc du Mont-Royal In the heart of Montréal, this park is especially fun for kids in winter, with tobogganing, skiing, snowshoeing and ice skating. (p80)

Best Rainy-day Activities

Cirque du Soleil The world-renowned show combines dance, theater and circus in power-packed summertime shows. (p43)

Biosphère Make a dam and walk on water at this hands-on multimedia museum in Parc Jean-Drapeau. (p47)

Biodôme Kids will love this giant indoor zoo with forest, river and marine habitats. (p89)

Planétarium Get a wide-eyed view of outer space at interactive exhibits and during shows in the domed theaters. (p89)

Insectarium The Insectarium (p89) has 250,000 specimens creeping, crawling or otherwise on display.

Top Travel Tips

Specialty Resources Exploring Montréal with Kids (www.montrealfamilies.ca).

Transport Up to five children under 11 can travel free accompanied by a paying adult on weekends (after 4pm Friday to end of Sunday). Children under six travel free.

LGBTIQ+

MEUNIERD/SHUTTERSTOCK ©

Montréal's gay community is centered in The Village, with loads of great cafes, restaurants, shops, bars and clubs. Québec City's gay community is tiny but well established, with its own Pride festival, the Fête Arc-en-Ciel, in early September and a handful of popular nightspots along Rue St-Jean in the St-Jean Baptiste district.

Best Nightspots

Sky Pub & Club (☎514-529-6969; www.complexesky.com; 1474 Rue Ste-Catherine Est; admission free; ⏰10pm-3am Thu-Sun, bar & roof 11am-late daily; Ⓜ Beaudry) A popular three-level Village complex designed for a Friday or Saturday night of partying. The roof terrace is a perfect place to catch fireworks in summer.

Aigle Noir (☎514-529-0040; 1315 Rue Ste-Catherine Est; ⏰8am-3am; Ⓜ Beaudry) A bar for the leather-and-fetish crowd where barmen are topless and porn plays on the screens.

Le Date Karaoke (www.ledatekaraoke.com; 1218 Rue Ste-Catherine Est; ⏰8am-3am; Ⓜ Beaudry) This gay tavern knew what it was doing when it added karaoke. A mixed crowd cheers aspiring vocalists from all walks of life.

Unity (http://clubunity.com; 1171 Rue Ste-Catherine Est; after 11pm Fri & Sat cover $8, Thu free; ⏰10pm-3am Thu-Sun; Ⓜ Beaudry) This three-floor Village favorite features a gay/mixed club and pub that has a VIP lounge, pool tables and rooftop terrace.

Le Drague (☎418-649-7212; www.ledrague.com; 815 Rue St-Augustin, St-Jean Baptiste; ⏰10am-3am) The star player on Québec City's tiny gay scene has an attractive outdoor terrace that is packed in summer, a stage for drag shows, and a more laid-back cocktail bar on the upper level.

Best Festivals

Montréal Pride (Fierté Montréal; ☎514-903-6193; http://fiertemtl.com; ⏰Aug) Largest pride week in Canada (pictured), culminating in the annual Montréal Pride Parade on René-Lévesque Boulevard.

Black & Blue Festival (☎514-875-7026; www.bbcm.org; ⏰Oct) One of Montréal's biggest gay events, with themed dance parties and art shows.

Fête Arc-en-Ciel (Québec City Pride Festival; ☎418-809-3383; www.arcencielquebec.ca; ⏰early Sep) This Québec City Gay Pride celebration draws more than 35,000 people for three nights of free shows in Place d'Youville and two days of entertainment on Rue St-Jean.

Under the Radar

Once you've hit the well-known blockbuster sites in Montréal and Québec City, hang out with the locals at lesser-known attractions, cool urban parks and vibrant, ever-changing smaller neighborhoods.

HEMIS/ALAMY STOCK PHOTO ©

Villeray, Montréal

All the ingredients for a charming neighborhood were already in Villeray – abundant green spaces, tree-lined streets, and a village vibe – but wonderful cafes and neighborhood restaurants have turned Villeray into the coolest place to hang out.

Local Québec Life

If historical tourism fatigue sets in while traipsing around Old Québec, get a glimpse of real life in St-Jean-Baptiste and St-Roch. Other towns where the village vibe has been rediscovered include working-class neighborhood St-Sauveur ('Saint-Sô' to locals) and Limoilu with its tree-lined streets and old brick homes.

Alternative Attractions

Montréal is jam-packed with under-the-radar visitor sites. Museum-wise, check out Écomusée du Fier Monde (pictured), an industrial history museum located in a vintage public bath house, or encounter cutting edge contemporary art at the brilliant Fonderie Darling. Over in Québec City, consider La Maison Henry-Stuart, a delightfully preserved house museum lined with antiques.

Green Spaces

Side-step the region's most crowded city parks and find peace in the quieter corners of Montréal's lovely Parc Outremont or the larger Westmount Park, a verdant swathe that's also home to a heritage public library. Then indulge in some birding and hiking (plus views of the famed swirling waters) at Parc des Rapides. For a Québec City respite, divert to the small Jardin des Gouverneurs, where you'll have tree-framed St. Lawrence River views.

Overtourism

Overtourism is a growing concern in Québec City where, before the pandemic, there were government plans to double cruise-ship visitor numbers by 2025.

The tourism board has tried to nip overtourism in the bud by creating neighborhood itineraries to encourage visitors to stray beyond Old Montréal. For some events that are popular with locals, the board does zero promotion to tourists, so it's worth speaking to a local to find out what's on.

Four Perfect Days

Day 1 – Montréal

KIEV.VICTOR/SHUTERSTOCK ©

Take the subway to Place-d'Armes and head for the **Basilique Notre-Dame** (p30). Explore the old town, strolling past **Place Jacques-Cartier** (p36), pictured, and up to the sailors' church, **Chapelle Notre-Dame-de-Bon-Secours** (p38).

Have lunch at the **Olive + Gourmando** (p39), then discover the city's history at the **Pointe-à-Callière Cité d'Archéologie et d'Histoire de Montréal** (p36). Visit **Fonderie Darling** (p37) for its contemporary-art installations.

Dine early at **Garde-Manger** (p40) or **Barroco** (p40), then see a play at the **Centaur Theatre** (p44), or **Cirque du Soleil** (p43). End with drinks on the rooftop patio at **Terrasse Place d'Armes** (p44).

Day 2 – Montréal

BAKERJARVIS/SHUTERSTOCK ©

Take an early morning stroll through **Parc du Mont-Royal** (p80) and admire the views from the **Belvédère Kondiaronk** (p87), pictured. Afterwards, descend to downtown's **Musée des Beaux-Arts de Montréal** (p52), and enjoy an excellent collection of Old Masters and contemporary art.

For lunch go to the **Marché Atwater** (p105). There you can pick up some excellent delicacies for a waterside picnic by the nearby **Canal de Lachine** (p102). Take a post-lunch bike ride on the canalside path.

That night, enjoy a Québécois feast at celebrated **Joe Beef** (p108). Afterwards, catch some live jazz at **Upstairs** (p64), or relax over drinks at **Dominion Square Tavern** (p62).

Day 3 – Montréal

BONDARENCO VLADIMIR/SHUTTERSTOCK ©

Make for Little Italy for morning espresso, followed by a wander through the **Marché Jean-Talon** (p91), pictured. Browse the old-world shops along Blvd St-Laurent before hopping a bus (or Bixi) to Mile End.

Have lunch at the charming little **Arts Cafe** (p94), then ramble along St-Viateur and Bernard, visiting **Drawn & Quarterly** (p99) for its whimsical book selections.

Continue the neighborhood exploring down in the Plateau, going cafe-hopping and window shopping along Ave du Mont-Royal and Rue St-Denis. That night, indulge in Montréal's best poutine at **La Banquise** (p80). Afterward, go on a late-night bar crawl down Blvd St-Laurent.

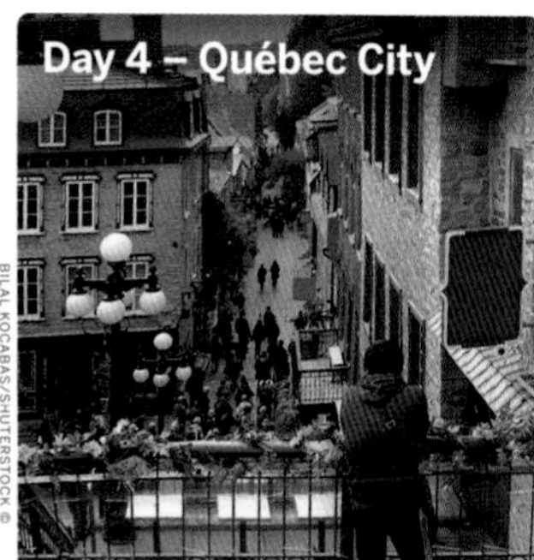

Day 4 – Québec City

BILAL KOCABAS/SHUTTERSTOCK ©

Wake up in Québec City! Spend the morning in the Old Town (pictured), taking in the views from the **Terrasse Dufferin** (p126), delving into the past at **Le Monastère des Augustines** (p126), and wandering the imposing corridors of **La Citadelle** (p116).

Have lunch at **Le Lapin Sauté** (p128), then stroll the cobblestone streets of the scenic Le Quartier Petit-Champlain neighborhood. Don't miss a visit to the incomparable **Musée de la Civilisation** (p120).

In the evening, head to the St-Jean Baptiste district, which has an excellent assortment of shops, restaurants, cafes and bars. Have dinner at **Buvette Scott** (p141) followed by drinks at **Le Sacrilège** (p142).

Need to Know

For detailed information, see Survival Guide (p145)

Languages
French, English

Currency
Canadian dollar ($)

Visas
Not required for citizens of Australia, New Zealand, United Kingdom and the United States, among others. See www.cic.gc.ca.

Money
ATMs are widely available. Major credit cards are widely accepted.

Mobile Phones
Buy local prepaid SIM cards for use with unlocked international phones.

Time
Eastern Time (GMT/UTC minus five hours)

Tipping
A tip of 15% of the pretax bill is customary in restaurants.

Daily Budget

Budget: less than $100

Dorm bed: $22–32

Supermarkets, markets, fast-food restaurants: $30

Movie tickets: $12

Midrange: $100–$200

Double room in a B&B: $130–180

Two-course dinner with glass of wine: $60

Theater ticket: $40

Top End: more than $200

Boutique hotel room: $200–350

Table d'hôte (fixed-price, multicourse meal) in deluxe restaurant with wine: $80

Canadiens de Montréal hockey ticket: $200

Advance Planning

Two months before Book tickets for hockey games, big concerts and major festivals, and make reservations for top restaurants.

Three weeks before Scan web listings for festivals and events; book hotels and specialized tours. Be sure to have adequate clothing for winter.

A few days before Check the weather at www.weather.gc.ca.

Arriving in Montréal & Québec City

Montréal-Pierre Elliott Trudeau International Airport

Buses ($10, one hour) and taxis ($40, 30 minutes) run to Downtown Montréal around the clock.

Gare Centrale, Montréal

Trains pulling into Montréal arrive at this Downtown terminus, with handy metro access to other parts of town.

Aéroport International Jean-Lesage de Québec

A taxi to the Old Town costs $35 (30 minutes); buses (2 hours) require a transfer.

Gare du Palais & Gare Routière de Québec

From the combined train and bus stations catch bus 1 to the Old Lower Town.

Getting Around

Montréal is Québec City's gateway and many travelers make the journey between the two by car, bus or rail. The drive is about three hours. VIA Rail's trains take only slightly longer (3¼ hours).

Bicycle

Montréal's popular Bixi bike-rental system (pictured) has more than 500 stations. Both cities have extensive bike-lane networks.

Bus

Both cities offer efficient and relatively cheap buses.

Metro

Montréal has an excellent metro system with four lines.

Taxi

Taxis are widely available.

Montréal Neighborhoods

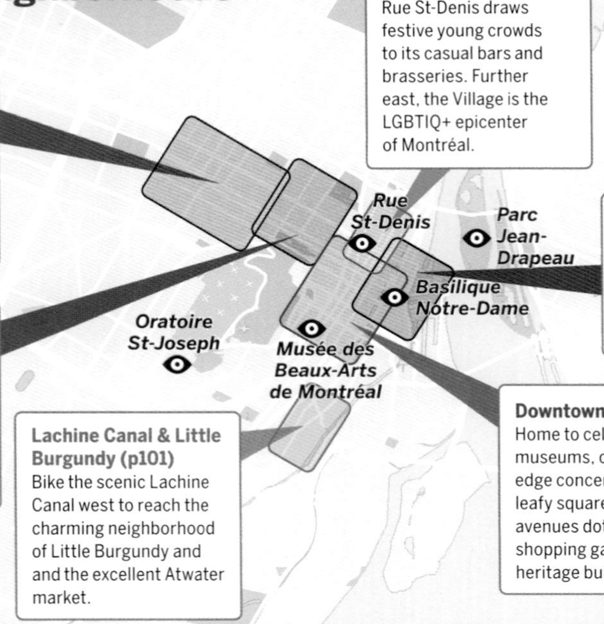

Little Italy, Mile End & Outremont (p91)
A foodie's dreamland, with new-wave eateries, old-school cafes and Montréal's biggest market. Quirky shops and creative bars add to the allure.

Plateau Mont-Royal (p75)
Bohemian district with vintage stores, restaurants and cocktail dens. Victorian-lined streets are great for exploring.

Lachine Canal & Little Burgundy (p101)
Bike the scenic Lachine Canal west to reach the charming neighborhood of Little Burgundy and and the excellent Atwater market.

Rue St-Denis & the Village (p67)
Rue St-Denis draws festive young crowds to its casual bars and brasseries. Further east, the Village is the LGBTIQ+ epicenter of Montréal.

Old Montréal (p29)
The historic heart of the city, with grand plazas, soaring cathedrals, and atmospheric lanes that invite endless exploring.

Downtown (p51)
Home to celebrated museums, cutting-edge concert halls, leafy squares and wide avenues dotted with shopping galleries and heritage buildings.

Explore Montréal

Combining urban sophistication with a French-derived appreciation of the good things in life, Montréal is home to old-world architecture, a thriving arts scence, frenetic nightlife and world-class dining options.

Montréal's Walking Tours

LA CAGE
AUX SPORTS
RESTO • BAR

Old Montréal

On the edge of St Lawrence River, historic Old Montréal is a place of picturesque squares, cobblestone streets and grand old-world architecture. Atmospheric lanes, like narrow Rue St-Paul, teem with art galleries, shops and eateries, while green parkland fronting river views define the Old Port. Nearby Chinatown is a small, wonderful dose of Pacific Rim cosmopolitanism in eastern Canada.

The Short List

- ***Basilique Notre-Dame (p30)*** *Soaking up the beautiful craftwork and soaring architecture of the city's spiritual jewel.*
- ***Old Port (p36)*** *Enjoying a circus performance, river cruise, or waterfront stroll along the St Lawrence.*
- ***Place d'Armes (p36)*** *Getting your bearings amid heritage architecture and a monument to Montréal's founder.*
- ***Pointe-à-Callière Cité d'archéologie et d'histoire de Montréal (p36)*** *Journeying back to Montréal's early foundation on a fascinating subterranean walk.*

Getting There & Around

M Take the metro to Square-Victoria, Place-d'Armes or Champ-de-Mars.

Bus 14 runs along Rue Notre-Dame in Old Montréal between Rue Berri and Blvd St-Laurent; bus 55 stops on Blvd St-Laurent.

A bike path along the Canal de Lachine connects the Old Port to the fringes of downtown at Rue Charlevoix.

Old Montréal Map on p34

Old Montréal RONNIE CHUA/SHUTTERSTOCK ©

Top Experience

Attend the Aura Basilica at Basilique Notre-Dame

This grand dame of Montréal's ecclesiastical treasures is a must-see when exploring the city. The looming Gothic Revival church can hold up to 3200 worshippers and houses a collection of finely crafted artworks, including an elaborately carved altarpiece, vibrant stained-glass windows and an intricate pulpit. All creating a canvas for the city's best multimedia lightshow.

MAP P34, C3

www.basiliquenotredame.ca

110 Rue Notre-Dame Ouest

adult/child $8/5

8am-4:30pm Mon-Fri, to 4pm Sat, 12:30-4pm Sun

M Place-d'Armes

History

The Sulpicians commissioned James O'Donnell, a New York architect and Irish Protestant, to design what would be the largest church north of Mexico. It opened in 1829. He converted to Catholicism so he could have his funeral in the basilica, and is buried in the crypt.

Design

The basilica has a spectacular interior with a forest of ornate wood pillars and carvings made entirely by hand (and constructed without the aid of a single nail), pictured. Gilt stars shine from the ceiling vaults and the altar is backlit in evening-sky blues. The stained glass windows are conspicuous for their depiction of events in Montréal's history rather than the usual biblical scenes.

The massive 7000-pipe **Casavant Frères organ** provides the powerful anthem at the famous Christmas concerts; the church bell, the Gros Bourdon, is the largest on the continent.

Wedding Chapel

The **Chapelle du Sacré Cœur**, located behind the main hall, is nicknamed the Wedding Chapel for the constant flow of couples tying the knot here. The curious mix of styles emerged after a 1978 fire, when the chapel was rebuilt with a brass altar with abstract-modern motifs.

Aura Basilica

A unique immersive multimedia show where the interior of the Basilique Notre-Dame becomes the canvas for a light show set to surging orchestral music. The columns, ceiling and statues seem to pulse with life as video and lasers are projected all around you in a dazzling 20-minute show. You also receive another 20 minutes to take in the basilica in a calmer light show. Reserve online.

★ Top Tips

- It's a picturesque, easy walk here from the Old Port.
- Walk down the adjacent side street to get a different view of the Basilique's exterior.
- For quiet prayer or some reflection away from the crowds, head to the small chapel in the rear.
- While there is an admission fee with an included tour, visiting for Mass is free.
- If taking photos is important, don't visit during a service, when photography is not allowed.

Take a Break

Nearby Kupfert & Kim (p39) has tasty meat- and wheat-free bowl food.

Continue the magnificent architecture with coffee at Crew Café (p42), housed in the former Royal Bank.

Walking Tour

Reliving History

One of Canada's most atmospheric neighborhoods, Old Montréal is packed with history. This stroll takes you back through the ages, along cobblestone lanes, across plazas and former marketplaces, against the backdrop of some of the city's first skyscrapers. Public art and striking architecture are also part of this Old Montréal stroll, as are fine perspectives from the city's most important history museum.

Walk Facts

Start Basilique Notre-Dame; M Place d'Armes

End Place d'Armes; M Place d'Armes

Length 2km; two hours

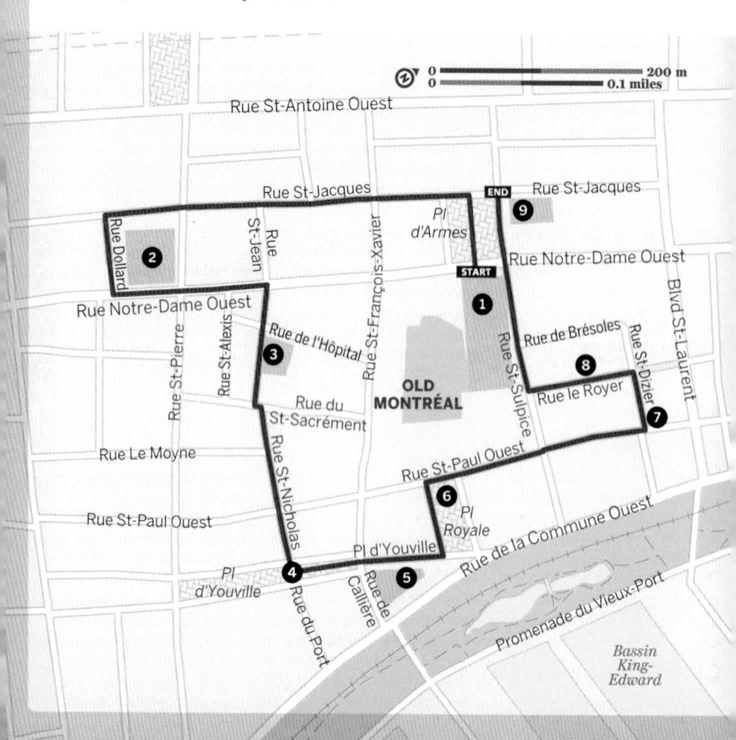

❶ Spiritual Icon

On the southeast side of Place d'Armes is the city's most celebrated cathedral, **Basilique Notre-Dame** (p30). Inside are a spectacularly carved pulpit and richly hued stained-glass windows relating key events from the city's founding.

❷ A 1920s Landmark

Cross the Place and head left along Rue St-Jacques, once known as Canada's Wall St. Stop at the grand **Royal Bank Tower** (Royal Bank Building; 360 Rue St-Jacques; admission free; 8am-8pm; M Square Victoria), Montréal's tallest edifice in 1928, to see its palatial interior, now the glorious Crew Cafe at the rear.

❸ Neo-Gothic Architecture

Loop back onto Rue Notre-Dame then right down Rue St-Jean. On the corner of Rue de l'Hôpital, the **Lewis Building** has dragons and gargoyles on the facade. It was built for Cunard Shipping Lines, a steamship company founded in 1840.

❹ A Picturesque Plaza

A few blocks further is **Place d'Youville**, one of Old Montréal's prettiest squares. Some of the first Europeans settled here in 1642 and an obelisk commemorates the city's founding.

❺ Montréal's Foundations

Nearby is fascinating **Pointe-à-Callière Cité d'archéologie et d'histoire de Montréal** (p36). Inside see the city's ancient foundations, or go to the top floor for fine views over the Old Port. Kids can board an interactive pirate ship to heave mast cranks and swing in hammocks in the sleeping quarters.

❻ Colonial Marketplace

Across the road is the Palladian-style 1836 **Old Customs House** (Vieille Douane; Pl Royale). It's in front of **Place Royale**, the early settlement's marketplace in the 17th and 18th centuries. Gaze up at the pediment to see the restored bas-relief figure of Albion, representing Britain.

❼ Art on the Streets

Walk right down Rue St-Paul to see the 2006 bronze sculpture *Les Chuchoteuses* (the Whisperers), tucked in a corner near Rue St-Dizier. This was one of many projects to revitalize the old quarter.

❽ Hidden Pedestrian Lane

Head up St-Dizier and turn left onto lovely **Cours Le Royer**, a tranquil pedestrian mall with fountains. On the north-side passageway is a stained-glass window of Jérôme Le Royer, one of Montréal's founders.

❾ First Skyscraper

Turn right on St-Sulpice and return to Place d'Armes. Note the **New York Life Building** (511 Pl d'Armes), Montréal's first skyscraper (1888), eight stories tall.

A B C D
1 2 3 4 5 6

Pl Phillips
Pl de la Paix
Rue Clark
Blvd René-Lévesque Ouest
Restaurant ChinaTown Kim Fung
24
Blvd St-Laurent
Rue Carmichael
Rue de Bleury
Rue Anderson
Rue Jeanne-Mance
Chinatown
5
Côte du Beaver Hall
Rue Belmont
Rue Dowd
13
Rue St-Urbain
Little Sheep Hot Pot
Rue de la Gauchetière Ouest
Square-Victoria
Pho Bang New York
Ave Viger Ouest
Place-d'Armes
Rue St-Alexandre
Place Jean-Paul-Riopelle
Autoroute Ville-Marie
9
20
Rue Square Victoria
Rue St-Antoine Ouest
Rlle des Fortifications
Sq Victoria
Rue St-François-Xavier
15
30
Rue St-Jacques
2 Place d'Armes
12
34
23
29
Basilique Notre-Dame
Rue Notre-Dame Ouest
21
Rue Ste-Hélène
22
Rue de l'Hôpital
31
Rue St-Sulpice
OLD MONTRÉAL
Rue St-Maurice
Rue de Longueuil
Rue McGill
Rue Le Moyne
19
27
32
25
14
Rue St-Paul Ouest
17
Pl Royale
33
18
Pl d'Youville
3
Rue William
Pointe-à-Callière Cité d'archéologie et d'histoire de Montréal
Rue Normand
Rue St-Pierre
16
6
Fonderie Darling
Conveyor Pier
Rue des Soeurs-Grises
Rue de la Commune Ouest
Rue Wellington
Rue Marguerite d'Youville
Promenade du Vieux-Port
Quai Alexandra
Rue King
Rue Queen
Rue Prince
26
Bota Bota
11
Bassin Alexandra
Parc des Écluses

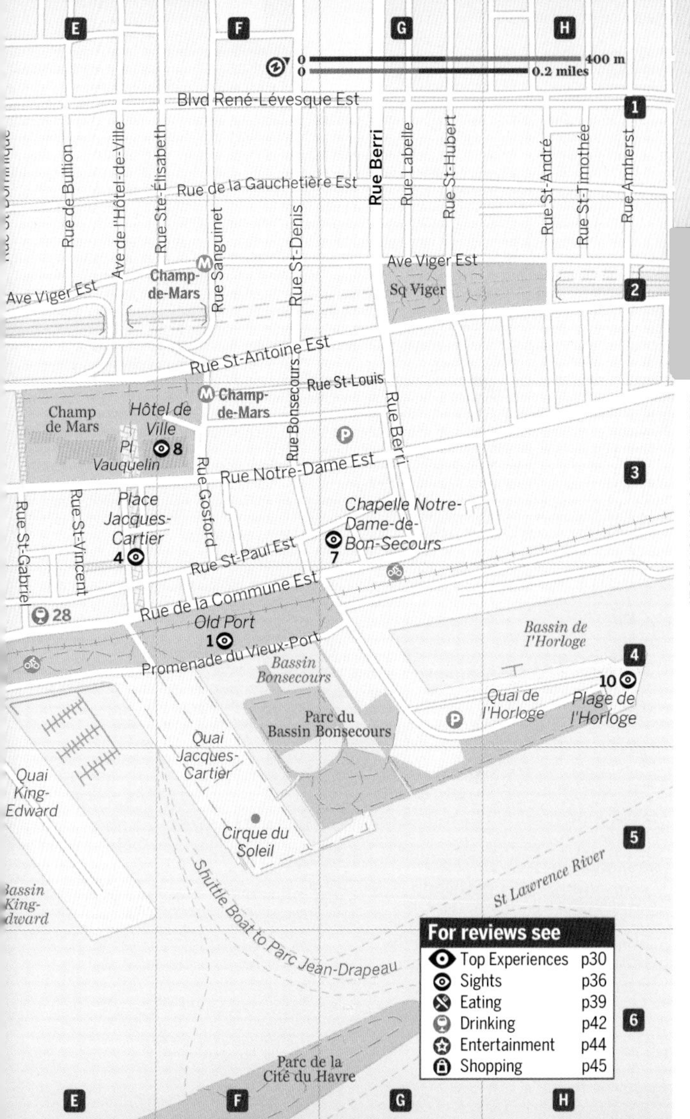

For reviews see

Top Experiences	p30
Sights	p36
Eating	p39
Drinking	p42
Entertainment	p44
Shopping	p45

Sights

Old Port PARK

1 MAP P34, F4

Montréal's Old Port has morphed into a park and fun zone paralleling the mighty St Lawrence River for 2.5km and punctuated by four grand *quais* (quays). Locals and visitors alike come here to enjoy strolling around, going for a cycle, or in-line skating. Cruise boats, ferries, jet boats and speedboats all depart for tours from various docks at the Old Port. In the winter months the Old Port is still worth a visit; you can cut a fine figure on an outdoor ice-skating rink (p44). (Vieux-Port de Montréal;)

Place d'Armes HISTORIC SITE

2 MAP P34, C3

This open square is framed by some of the finest buildings in all of Old Montréal, including its oldest bank, its very first skyscraper and the stunning Basilique Notre-Dame (p30). The square's name references the bloody battles that took place here as religious settlers and indigenous groups clashed over control of what would later become Montréal. At its center stands the **Monument Maisonneuve**, dedicated to city founder Paul de Chomedey, *sieur* de Maisonneuve. (M Place-d'Armes)

Pointe-à-Callière Cité d'archéologie et d'histoire de Montréal MUSEUM

3 MAP P34, C4

One of Montréal's most fascinating sites, this museum takes visitors on a historical journey through the centuries, beginning with the early days of the city. Visitors should start with *Yours Truly, Montréal*, an 18-minute multimedia show that covers the arrival of the Amerindians, the founding of Montréal and other key moments, and will give you a good overview before you venture further into the museum. Afterward, head to the **archaeological crypt** where you can explore the remains of the city's ancient sewerage and river system, and the foundations of its first buildings and public square. (Museum of Archaeology & History; 514-872-9150; www.pacmuseum.qc.ca; 350 Pl Royale; adult/child $22/8; 10am-5pm Tue-Fri, from 11am Sat & Sun; ; M Place-d'Armes)

Place Jacques-Cartier SQUARE

4 MAP P34, E3

The liveliest spot in Old Montréal, this gently inclined square hums with performance artists, street musicians and the animated chatter from terrace restaurants lining its borders. A public market was set up here after a château burned down in 1803. At its top end stands the **Colonne Nelson**, a monument erected to Admiral Lord Nelson after his defeat of Napoleon's fleet at Trafalgar. (admission free; M Champ-de-Mars)

Chinatown

AREA

5 MAP P34, D2

Although this neighborhood, perfectly packed into a few easily navigable streets, has no sites per se, it's a nice area for going for lunch, or for a spot of shopping for quirky knickknacks. The main thoroughfare, Rue de la Gauchetière, between Blvd St-Laurent and Rue Jeanne-Mance, is enlivened with Taiwanese bubble-tea parlors, Hong Kong–style bakeries and Vietnamese soup restaurants. The public square, **Place Sun-Yat-Sen** (M Place-d'Armes), attracts teenagers, crowds of older people and the occasional group of Falun Gong practitioners.

Fonderie Darling

ARTS CENTER

6 MAP P34, A5

Tucked away in a little-visited corner of Old Montréal, the Darling Foundry hosts avant-garde, often large-scale exhibitions and installations in its two sizable showrooms. The brick industrial building, which dates all the way back to the early 1900s, once housed a prosperous iron foundry and is today home to the gallery and live-work studios for artists. (514-392-1554; www.fonderiedarling.org; 745 Rue Ottawa; $5, Thu free; noon-7pm Wed & Fri-Sun, to 10pm Thu; M Square-Victoria)

Old Port

Chapelle Notre-Dame-de-Bon-Secours CHURCH

7 MAP P34, G3

Known as the Sailors' Church, this enchanting chapel derives its name from the sailors who left behind votive lamps in the shapes of ships in thanksgiving for safe passage. The restored interior has stained-glass windows and paintings depicting key moments in the life of the Virgin Mary (for whom Montréal – aka Ville-Marie – was originally named). The attached **Musée Marguerite-Bourgeoys** relates the story of Montréal's first teacher and the founder of the Congregation of Notre-Dame order of nuns. (514-282-8670; https://margueritebourgeoys.org; 400 Rue St-Paul Est; chapel free, museum adult/student/child $12/9/7; 10am-6pm Tue-Sun May-Oct, 11am-4pm Tue-Sun Nov–mid-Jan & Mar-Apr; ; M Champ-de-Mars)

Hôtel de Ville HISTORIC BUILDING

Montréal's handsome City Hall was built between 1872 and 1878, then rebuilt after a fire in 1926. Its rigid square-based dome and nod to the baroque makes it a fine example of Second Empire–style architecture. It's steeped in local lore: in 1967 French leader Charles de Gaulle famously yelled from its balcony to the crowds outside '*Vive le Québec libre!*' ('Long live free Québec!'). Those four words fueled the fires of Québécois separatism and strained relations with Ottawa for years. (City Hall; 275 Rue Notre-Dame Est; admission free; 8:30am-5pm Mon-Fri; M Champ-de-Mars)

Place Jean-Paul-Riopelle SQUARE

The big draw of this square by the Palais Des Congrès is the **fountain** that releases a ring of fire (and an ethereal mist) at certain times of year. The fountain and sculpture by Jean-Paul Riopelle (1923–2002), called *La Joute* (The Joust), was inaugurated here in 2003. During the day this area is filled with nearby office workers having lunch, but summer nights are a big draw – that's when the pyrotechnics take place. (ring of fire hourly 6:30-10:30pm mid-May–mid-Oct; M Place-d'Armes)

Plage de l'Horloge BEACH

Montréal opened this 'urban beach' along the Quai de l'Horloge in 2012, trucking in sand, Adirondack chairs, parasols and a bar. Unfortunately, there's no swimming, but it's a fine spot to take in views of the river and to catch some rays. (www.oldportofmontreal.com/activity/clock-tower-beach; fireworks evenings $5; 11am-7pm Mon-Wed, to 9pm Thu-Sun, to 11pm fireworks evenings late Jun-early Sep; M Champ-de-Mars)

Bota Bota

SPA

11 MAP P34, C6

This unique floating spa is actually a 1950s ferry that's been repurposed as an oasis on the water. It's permanently docked by the Old Port with great city views, offering a range of treatments on its five beautifully redesigned decks. The Water Circuit admission (from $40) gives you access to saunas, hot tubs and the outdoor terraces. (514-284-0333; www.botabota.ca; 358 Rue de la Commune Ouest; 10am-10pm, from 9am Fri-Sun; M Square-Victoria)

Eating

Kupfert & Kim

VEGETARIAN $

12 MAP P34, B3

Toronto's stylish yet well-priced vegetarian bowls bring the same health-conscious focus to Montréal without losing any of the flavor, while creating an exemplar for quick food in Old Montréal. Nearly everything is made from scratch, even sauces. Standouts are the sweet-potato curry with brown rice, the 'rainbow bowl' of shredded vegetables, and smoothie bowls. (www.kupfertandkim.com; 417 Rue Notre-Dame Oest; mains $10-15; 10am-8pm; ; M Square-Victoria)

Orange Rouge

ASIAN $$

13 MAP P34, C2

Hidden down a narrow lane of Chinatown, Orange Rouge has a quaint, low-lit interior that's rather nondescript save for the bright open kitchen at one end and a neon-lit crab sculpture on the wall. Grab a seat at the dark lacquered bar or on one of the banquettes for a feast of Asian fusion. (514-861-1116; www.orangerouge.ca; 106 de la Gauchetière Ouest; mains $15-20; 11:30am-2:30pm Tue-Fri & 5:30-10:30pm Tue-Sat; M Place-d'Armes)

Rue St-Paul Ouest

This narrow cobblestone street, the oldest in Montréal, was once a dirt road packed tight by horses laden with goods bound for the Old Port. Today it's a shopping street with galleries, boutiques and restaurants, touristy in spots but undeniably picturesque and enjoyable to wander.

Olive + Gourmando

CAFE $$

14 MAP P34, B4

Named after the owners' two cats, this bakery-cafe is legendary in town for its hot panini, generous salads and flaky baked goods. Excellent choices include the melted goat's-cheese panini with caramelized onions, decadent mac 'n' cheese, and 'the Cubain' (a ham, roast pork and Gruyère sandwich). Try to avoid the busy lunch rush (11:30am to 1:30pm). (514-350-1083; www.oliveetgourmando.com; 351 Rue St-Paul Ouest; mains $11-18; 8am-5pm Sun-Fri, to 6pm-Sat; ; M Square-Victoria)

Invitation V
VEGAN **$$**

15 MAP P34, C3

A game-changer in the world of vegan cuisine, Invitation V serves up creative, beautifully presented dishes in an elegant dining room of white brick and light woods. Start with butternut squash and roasted-red-pepper soup and a round of mushroom satay with peanut sauce, before moving onto curry stew with jasmine rice or a tempeh burger with sweet-potato fries. (514-271-8111; 201 Rue St-Jacques; mains $15-24; 10:30am-3pm Tue-Sun, 5:30-10pm Tue, Wed & Sat, to midnight Thu & Fri; ; M Place-d'Armes)

Le Serpent
ITALIAN **$$**

16 MAP P34, A5

Industrial style dominates at this renovated factory next to the Fonderie Darling (p37) art space, which draws a creative tech-industry crowd. The menu features an interesting mix of risottos and pastas (such as *bucatini* with pork confit) and a handful of well-executed seafood and meat dishes (veal fillet with ricotta tortellini), plus a changing daily special. (514-316-4666; www.leserpent.ca; 257 Rue Prince; mains $13-35; 5:45-10:30pm Mon-Wed, to 11pm Thu & Fri, 5-11pm Sat; M Square-Victoria)

Stash Café
POLISH **$$**

17 MAP P34, C4

Hearty Polish cuisine is served up with good humor in a dining room with seats made of church pews and daringly low red lights illuminating the tables. It dishes out consistently quality traditional fare such as pierogi (dumplings stuffed with meat or cheese, with sour cream) and potato pancakes with apple sauce. A live piano player often adds atmosphere. (514-845-6611; http://restaurantstashcafe.ca; 200 Rue St-Paul Ouest; mains $15-25; 11:30am-10pm Sun-Thu, to 11pm Fri & Sat; M Place-d'Armes)

Barroco
INTERNATIONAL **$$$**

18 MAP P34, B4

Small, cozy Barroco has stone walls, flickering candles and beautifully presented plates of roast guinea fowl, paella, braised short ribs and grilled fish. The selection is small (just six or so mains and an equal number of appetizers), but you can't go wrong here – particularly if you opt for the outstanding seafood and chorizo paella. (514-544-5800; www.barroco.ca; 312 Rue St-Paul Ouest; mains $27-41; 5-10:30pm Sun-Wed, to 11pm Thu, to midnight Fri & Sat; M Square-Victoria)

Garde-Manger
INTERNATIONAL **$$$**

19 MAP P34, C4

The buzz surrounding Garde-Manger has barely let up since its opening back in 2006. This small, candlelit restaurant attracts a mix of local scenesters and *haute cuisine*–loving out-of-towners who come for lobster risotto, short ribs, Cornish hen stuffed with foie gras and other changing chalkboard specials. The stage is set with stone walls, great cocktails and a decidedly not-stuffy vibe. (☎514-678-5044; www.crownsalts.com/gardemanger; 408 Rue St-François-Xavier; mains $34-40; ⏰5:30-11pm Tue-Sun; Ⓜ Place-d'Armes)

Toqué! FRENCH $$$

20 MAP P34, B3

Chef Normand Laprise has earned rave reviews for his innovative recipes based on products sourced from local farms. The bright, wide-open dining room has high ceilings accented by playful splashes of color, and a glass-enclosed wine cave with suspended bottles looming. The seven-course *menu dégustation* ($142) is the pinnacle of dining in Montréal – allow three hours for the feast. (☎514-499-2084; www.restaurant-toque.com; 900 Pl Jean-Paul-Riopelle; mains $48-58; ⏰11:30am-1:45pm Tue-Fri, 5:30-10pm Tue-Thu, to 10:30pm Fri & Sat; Ⓜ Square-Victoria)

Tapas 24 SPANISH $$$

21  MAP P34, B3

Celebrated Catalan chef Carles Abellan brings a bit of Barcelona magic to the new world with this outstanding addition to Old Montréal – his first foray outside of Spain. Mouthwatering dishes include razor clams, garlic shrimp, Galician-style octopus and Iberian ham, as well as heartier plates of *fideua* (Catalan-style paella). (420 Notre-Dame Ouest; tapas $6-20, mains $25-48; ⏰5-11pm Tue-Sat, also 11:30am-2:30pm Thu & Fri; Ⓜ Square-Victoria)

Le Serpent

Chinatown Dining

A few blocks from the cobblestones of Old Montréal, you'll find the the tiny but lively Chinatown. It's home to a delectable assortment of bustling Cantonese, Vietnamese and even Mongolian eateries sprinkled along Blvd St-Laurent and the pedestrian Rue de la Gauchetière.

For a satisfying bowl of pho (Vietnamese noodle soup), stop in **Pho Bang New York** (Map p34, D2; ☎514-954-2032; https://phobangnewyork.com; 1001 Blvd St-Laurent; mains $9-16; ⏰10am-9:30pm; Ⓜ Place-d'Armes).

Dim sum lovers flock to **Restaurant ChinaTown Kim Fung** (Map p34, D1; ☎514-878-2888; www.restaurantchinatownkimfung.com; 1111 Rue St-Urbain; mains $10-16; ⏰7am-3pm & 4:30-10pm; Ⓜ Place-d'Armes), which is a popular weekend brunch spot.

At **Little Sheep Hot Pot** (Map p34, D2; 50 Rue de la Gauchetière Est; all-you-can-eat lunch/dinner $16/22; ⏰11am-10pm Mon-Thu, to 10:30pm Fri & Sat; Ⓜ Place-d'Armes), you pick your ingredients, and cook them up tableside in the simmering hot pot.

L'Orignal

QUÉBÉCOIS $$$

22 MAP P34, B3

This cozy chalet-style restaurant specializes in exquisitely prepared game meat and fresh seafood. Start your dining experience off with the oysters or the venison-heart tartare before moving on to braised wild boar or crusted cod with caviar. The service is excellent and the cedar-filled dining room is a great spot to linger over what is sure to be a memorable meal. (☎514-303-0479; www.restaurant-lorignal.com; 479 Rue St-Alexis; mains $22-37; ⏰6-11pm; Ⓜ Place-d'Armes)

Drinking

Crew Café

CAFE

23 MAP P34, B3

Easily the most spectacular cafe in all of Montréal, Crew converted the old Royal Bank into a caffeine and laptop powerhouse. Order from a teller, then sip on a green tea or enjoy a good latte at a gilded deposit-slip table (remember deposit slips?) while gazing way up at the ornate ceiling laden with chandeliers. It's worth popping in just to have a gander, especially for architecture and interior-design fans. (http://crewcollectivecafe.com; 360 Rue St-Jacques; ⏰8am-8pm; 📶; Ⓜ Square-Victoria)

Le Mal Necessaire COCKTAIL BAR

24 MAP P34, D1

For some of the tastiest cocktails in Montréal, look for the neon-lit green pineapple and descend the stairs to this vaguely Tiki-inspired bar hidden along pedestrian-filled St Laurent. Fruity elixirs are tops – especially the Abacaxi mai tai, served in a pineapple – whipped up by friendly bartenders. (www.lemalnecessaire.com; 1106 Blvd St-Laurent; 4:30pm-2am Sun-Wed, to 3am Thu-Sat; M St-Laurent)

Flyjin COCKTAIL BAR

25 MAP P34, B4

Flyjin walks a fine line between speakeasy and high-end Asian brasserie, serving up tender sashimi, tuna tataki and green papaya salad, and finely crafted cocktails (like sake mojitos and cachaça–dragon fruit combos) to a party-minded crowd. It has a barely marked entrance, leading down to the subterranean – but beautifully designed – space. (514-564-8881; www.flyjinmtl.com; 417 Rue St-Pierre; 7pm-3am Wed-Sat; M Square-Victoria)

Les Sœurs Grises PUB

26 MAP P34, B5

Named after the famous Montréal religious order of nuns founded by St Marguerite d'Youville, this swanky concrete-chic bistro-brasserie is equal parts microbrewery and smokehouse, serving a winning combination of brews and bites. Grab some smoked baby-back ribs, candied pheasant thighs or smoked trout, and wash it down with excellent house beers and silky stouts. (514-788-7635; www.bblsg.com; 32 Rue McGill; noon-midnight Mon-Thu, 11:30am-3am Fri & Sat, 3pm-midnight Sun; M Square-Victoria)

Philémon CLUB

27  MAP P34, D4

A major stop for local scenesters rotating between watering holes in the old city, Philémon was carved out of stone, brick and wood with large windows looking out over Rue St-Paul. Twenty-somethings fill the space around a huge central bar sipping basic cocktails and nibbling on light fare (oysters, charcuterie plates, smoked-meat sandwiches), while a DJ spins house and hip-hop. (514-289-3777; www.philemonbar.com; 111 Rue St-Paul Ouest; 5pm-3am Mon-Wed, from 4pm Thu & Fri, from 6pm Sat & Sun; M Place-d'Armes)

Cirque du Soleil

Globally famous **Cirque du Soleil** (Map p35, F5; www.cirquedusoleil.com; tickets from $67; M Champ-de-Mars), one of the city's most famous exports, puts on a new production of acrobats and music in a marvelous tent complex in the old port roughly once every two years in summer. These shows rarely disappoint, so don't pass up a chance to see one on its home turf.

Taverne Gaspar

PUB

28 MAP P34, E4

Facing the Old Port, this cozy watering hole in the Auberge du Vieux Port has faux-retro decor, a long zinc bar, and lobster sliders, oysters, and mac 'n' cheese. The house brew is the Gaspar lager. There's live music on Wednesday evenings. (www.tavernegaspar.com; 89 Rue de la Commune Est; 7-11am & 5-10pm Sun-Wed, to 11pm Thu-Sat; M Champ-de-Mars)

L'Assommoir

PUB

29 MAP P34, C3

Like its sister pub in Mile End, L'Assommoir is home to a beautiful long bar that makes a great place to start the night with a house cocktail such as the GHB (gin, chartreuse, kiwi, maple syrup and a bit of apple and pear juice) and a few snacks (fried calamari or mixed ceviche). (www.assommoir.ca; 211 Rue Notre-Dame Ouest; 3pm-1am Sun-Wed, to 3am Thu-Sat; M Place-d'Armes)

Promenade du Vieux-Port

In warm weather the Old Port Promenade is a favorite recreation spot for joggers and in-line skaters, while cyclists can take in the view from the city bike path that runs parallel to it. There is plenty of green space for those seeking relaxation or phenomenal views of the L'International des Feux Loto-Québec. In winter, enjoy skating at the outdoor **patinoire (rink)** (Parc du Bassin Bonsecours; adult/child $6/4, skate rental $7; 10am-9pm Mon-Wed, to 10pm Thu-Sun; 14, M Champ-de-Mars), with the St Lawrence River shimmering nearby.

Terrasse Place d'Armes

BAR

30 MAP P34, D3

The rooftop terrace above the boutique Hôtel Place-d'Armes is a requisite stop on the nightlife circuit if you're around during the summer. Cocktails, eclectic cuisine and a fantastic view over Place d'Armes and the Basilique Notre-Dame (p30) never fail to bring in the crowd. (514-904-1201; www.terrasseplacedarmes.com; 8th fl, 710 Côte de la Pl d'Armes; 11am-3am summer; M Place-d'Armes)

Entertainment

Centaur Theatre

THEATER

31 MAP P34, C4

Montréal's chief English-language theater presents everything from Shakespearean classics to works by experimental Canadian playwrights. It occupies Montréal's former stock exchange (1903), a striking building with classical columns. (514-288-3161; www.centaurtheatre.com; 453 Rue St-François-Xavier; M Place-d'Armes)

GENEVIEVE TANGUAY-LEDUC ©

Espace Pepin

Shopping

Galerie LeRoyer

ART

32 MAP P34, D4

This spacious old gallery is at the forefront of the avant-garde scene in Montréal, previously under the moniker of Galerie St-Dizier. Works are split between local and heavyweight artists including Besner and Tetro. (GLR24; 514-845-8411; www.galerieleroyer.com; 24 Rue St-Paul Ouest; 10am-6pm Mon-Sun; M Champ-de-Mars)

Espace Pepin

HOMEWARES

33 MAP P34, B4

Boasting a vintage-chic aesthetic, Espace Pepin is a fun place to browse. You'll find wood-branch pepper and spice mills, elegant glassware, and baskets of handwoven hemp. A few doors down (at 350 Rue St-Paul Ouest) is Pepin's fashion store, with high-end clothing and accessories. (514-844-0114; www.thepepinshop.com; 378 Rue St-Paul Ouest; 10am-6pm Mon-Sat, 11am-5pm Sun; M Square-Victoria)

Rooney

FASHION & ACCESSORIES

34 MAP P34, B3

Rooney is an inviting shop with stylish streetwear. You'll find Rag & Bone button-downs, Levis Vintage jackets and jeans, classic Chuck Taylors, Mismo wallets, Filson duffles and a table of fashion mags. (514-543-6234; www.rooneyshop.com; 395 Rue Notre-Dame Ouest; 11:30am-6pm Mon-Wed, to 8pm Thu & Fri, noon-5pm Sat & Sun; M Square-Victoria)

Top Experience

Stroll Through the Leafy Islands of Parc Jean-Drapeau

Worlds away from the city bustle, this park stretches across two leafy islands in the midst of the mighty St Lawrence, about half a mile east of the Old Port. The prime draws are outdoor activities such as cycling and jogging, though you'll also find some noteworthy museums, plus lake swimming and weekly dance parties in the summer.

MAP P49

www.parcjeandrapeau.com

Biosphère

Housed in Buckminster Fuller's striking geodesic dome (pictured) built for the American pavilion at Expo 67 World's Fair, this **nature center** (514-283-5000; www.ec.gc.ca/biosphere; adult/child $15/free, 25% discount with MuséeStewart ticket; 10am-5pm Jun-Nov, Wed-Sun Dec-May; M Jean-Drapeau) has its own geothermal energy system and fun interactive displays involving hand pumps and waterspouts. Exhibits focus on urban ecosystems and emerging ecotechnologies; there's a model house outside built using sustainable design principles. Explanations are good (though geared towards older children rather than young kids). The upstairs gallery about Fuller, and the exterior belvederes, offer spectacular river views.

Musée Stewart

Inside the old Arsenal British garrison (where troops were stationed in the 19th century), this beautifully renovated **museum** (514-861-6701; www.stewart-museum.org; 20 Chemin du Tour de l'Île; adult/child $15/free; 10am-5pm Tue-Sun Jul-Sep, Wed-Sun Oct-Jun) displays relics from Canada's past in its permanent exhibition, *History and Memory*. In summer, there are military parades outside by actors in 18th-century uniforms; check the website for details. It's a 1km (about 15-minute) walk from Jean-Drapeau metro station.

L'Homme

This huge **sculpture** (Humankind; M Jean-Drapeau) was created by famed artist Alexander Calder for Expo 67. Exit the metro and take the left/west path, which is well-signposted to take you the 400m to the sculpture.

★ Top Tips

- Musée Stewart has good views across the island and to the mainland.
- Prebook tickets for La Ronde during the summer-evening fireworks season.
- Winter is very quiet in the park, when all but Musée Stewart will be closed. You may find you have the snow-covered trees to yourself and the red foxes.

Take a Break

Dining options are limited; pick up some picnic fare before heading over to the island.

★ Getting There

M Jean-Drapeau.

777 (Casino) and 767/769 (La Ronde) link the islands.

Pont (Bridge) Jacques Cartier for Île Ste-Hélèn; Pont de la Concorde for Île Notre-Dame.

From the Old Port.

La Ronde

Québec's largest amusement park, **La Ronde** (514-397-2000; www.laronde.com; 22 Chemin Macdonald; season pass $42; hours vary May-Oct; P; M Jean-Drapeau) has a battery of impressive rides, including Le Monstre, the world's highest double wooden roller coaster, and Le Vampire, a corkscrew roller coaster with gut-wrenching turns. For a more peaceful experience, there's a Ferris wheel and a gentle minirail.

Concerts and shows are held throughout the summer; fireworks explode in July and early August on Wednesday and Saturday evenings (when the park stays open later).

Water Fun

More active families and travelers head to the **Complexe Aquatique** (www.parcjeandrapeau.com; adult/child $7.50/3.50; 10am-8pm daily early Jun-late Aug, noon-7pm daily late Aug-early Sep, noon-7pm Sat & Sun late May-early Jun; M Jean-Drapeau) just near the metro, for a summer splash. An outdoor dip with the sounds of birdlife around you is a special Parc Jean-Drapeau moment.

For more aquatic fun, head to **Plage Jean-Doré** (Plage des Îles; www.parcjeandrapeau.com; adult/child $9/4.50; 10am-7pm daily mid-Jun–late Aug, noon-7pm Sat-Mon late Aug-early Sep; M Jean-Drapeau, then bus 767), an artificial sandy beach on Île Notre-Dame. It's safe, clean and ideal for kids; picnic facilities and snack bars serving beer are on-site. There are also paddleboats, canoes and kayaks for rent.

Festivals & Events

Held on summer Sundays, **Piknic Électronik** (http://piknicelectronik.com; Pl de l'Homme; $14.50; 2-9pm Sun mid-May–late Sep; M Jean-Drapeau) features DJs spinning techno and electronic music. Going since 2006, **Osheaga Festival Musique et Arts** (www.osheaga.com; Pl de l'Homme; from $325; Aug) is the island's major music festival, showcasing local alternative bands and big international acts. **Heavy Montréal** (www.heavymontreal.com; Parc Jean-Drapeau; from $175; Aug) brings together metal and hard-rock lovers in August. **ÎleSoniq** (www.ilesoniq.com; Parc Jean-Drapeau; from $210; Aug), is an electronic-music fest also held in August.

Mainly on weekends from late June to early August, **L'International des Feux Loto-Québec** (Montréal Fireworks Festival; 10pm Wed & Sat Jul-early Aug) fireworks at La Ronde amusement park light up the skies.

Over four weekends from mid January to early February, you can enjoy the **Fête des Neiges** (514-872-6120; www.parcjeandrapeau.com; Parc Jean-Drapeau; admission free; 10am-5pm Sat & Sun late Jan–early Feb). This family-friendly event features ice sculpting, horse-drawn sleigh rides, dogsledding (humane-regulated by MAPAQ), ice skating, tubing and zip lines, plus shows and concerts.

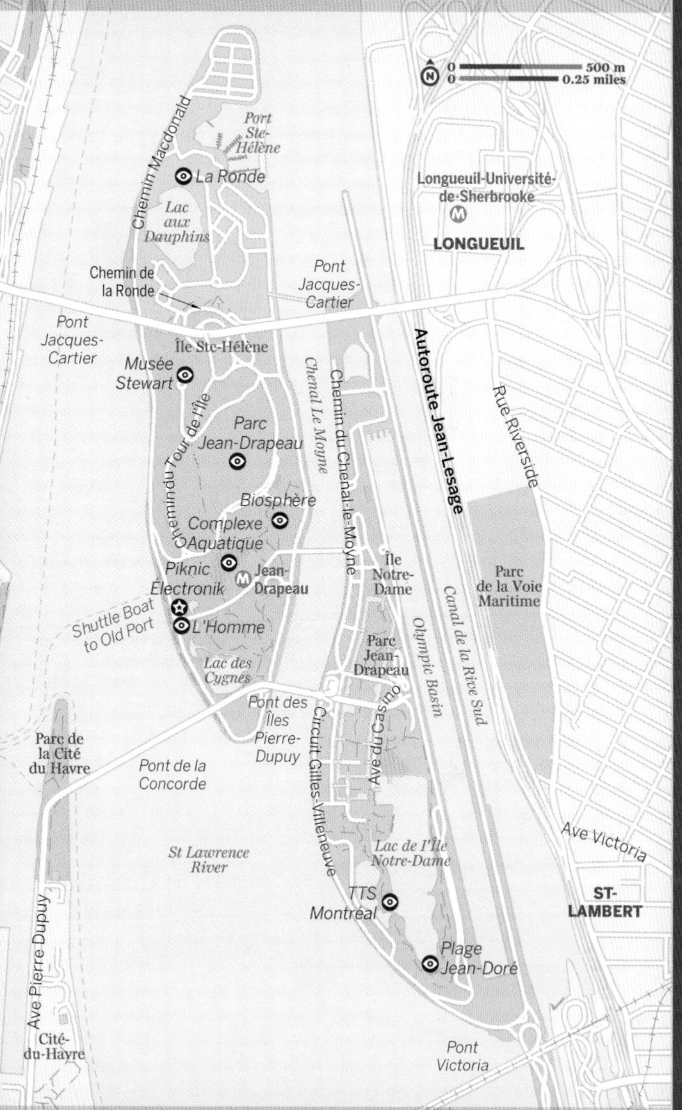
0 500 m
0 0.25 miles
Port Ste-Hélène
Chemin Macdonald
La Ronde
Lac aux Dauphins
Chemin de la Ronde
Pont Jacques-Cartier
Pont Jacques-Cartier
Longueuil-Université-de-Sherbrooke
LONGUEUIL
Île Ste-Hélène
Musée Stewart
Chemin du Tour de l'Île
Parc Jean-Drapeau
Chenal Le Moyne
Chemin du Chenal-le-Moyne
Autoroute Jean-Lesage
Rue Riverside
Biosphère
Complexe Aquatique
Piknic Électronik
Jean-Drapeau
Île Notre-Dame
Parc de la Voie Maritime
Shuttle Boat to Old Port
L'Homme
Lac des Cygnes
Parc Jean-Drapeau
Canal de la Rive Sud
Olympic Basin
Pont des Îles Pierre-Dupuy
Ave du Casino
Parc de la Cité du Havre
Pont de la Concorde
Circuit Gilles-Villeneuve
Ave Victoria
St Lawrence River
Lac de l'Île Notre-Dame
TTS Montréal
ST-LAMBERT
Ave Pierre Dupuy
Plage Jean-Doré
Cité-du-Havre
Pont Victoria

Explore

Downtown

Sprinkled amid skyscrapers and condo developments lie heritage buildings and old-time mansions, top-notch museums and numerous green spaces. The two most common groups here are businesspeople and students from McGill and Concordia Universities. The city's major shopping district is downtown, as is the performing-arts complex, Place des Arts. This is the epicenter of the city's jazz festival in the summer.

The Short List

- ***Musée des Beaux-Arts de Montréal (p52)*** *Spending a few hours exploring a treasure trove of traditional and contemporary art.*
- ***Place des Arts (p58)*** *Getting your festival freak on with thousands of others when the jazz festival hits the town.*
- ***Cathédrale Marie-Reine-du-Monde (p60)*** *Enjoying quiet time inside one of downtown's many beautiful historic churches.*
- ***Rue Sherbrooke Ouest (p60)*** *Browsing this street's eye-catching boutiques and heritage buildings.*

Getting There & Around

M Peel and McGill are both central and convenient.

Bus 15 runs on Rue Ste-Catherine and Blvd de Maisonneuve, bus 24 on Rue Sherbrooke and bus 150 on Blvd René-Lévesque.

Bixi bikes have numerous stations in the area. If you're cycling, Blvd de Maisonneuve has separate protected bike lanes.

Downtown Map on p56

Downtown Montréal

Top Experience

Visit Canada's Oldest Museum: Musée des Beaux-Arts de Montréal

Montréal's Museum of Fine Arts is an accessible and beautiful oasis of art housed in architecturally striking buildings. This is Canada's oldest museum and the city's largest, with works from Old Masters to contemporary artists. Special exhibitions have included the world premiere of works by fashion designer Thierry Mugler.

MAP P56, A3

www.mbam.qc.ca

1380 Rue Sherbrooke Ouest

exhibitions & pavilions $24/16/free

10am-5pm Tue-Sun, to 9pm Wed special exhibitions only

The Main Collection

The collection is housed in five pavilions. The beaux-arts, marble-covered **Michal & Renata Hornstein Pavilion** (www.mbam.qc.ca; 1379 Rue Sherbrooke Ouest; all Musée exhibitions & pavilions adult over 30yr/21-30yr/under 20yr $24/16/free, after 5pm Wed special exhibition $12; 10am-5pm, Tue-Sun, to 9pm Wed special exhibitions only; M Guy-Concordia) presents World Cultures – everything from ancient African to modern Japanese art.

Behind this building is the Liliane & David M Stewart Pavilion (pictured), with an eye-catching decorative-arts collection. Glass, ceramics, textiles, furniture and industrial design pieces from around the globe have been assembled here.

Adjacent to this building on Rue Bishop is the Michal & Renata Hornstein Pavilion for Peace (not to be confused with the similarly named pavilion mentioned above), which opened in 2017 and features 750 works from Old Masters to contemporary artists, and the Michel de la Chenelière International Atelier for Education and Art Therapy.

Canadian & Québécois Art

Across Ave du Musée, the Claire & Marc Bourgie Pavilion is situated in a renovated 1894 church and displays some magnificent works of Canadian and Québécois art. Head to the top floor to delve into Inuit art and its cultural legacy. The church's Bourgie Concert Hall features gorgeous Tiffany stained-glass windows and live shows.

Old & Modern Masters

The modern Moshe Safdie–designed annex across Sherbrooke is the Jean-Noël Desmarais Pavilion, home to the Old and Modern Masters, with paintings from the Middle Ages stretching through the Renaissance and classical eras up to contemporary works. It can be reached via an underground passage from the Hornstein Pavilion.

★ Top Tips

- Admission to the special exhibitions are usually half price on Wednesday after 5pm; general admission and Discovery exhibitions (but not the major exhibition) are free on the first Sunday of the month.
- Plan in lots of breaks or multiple visits. There is lots of walking to be done so trying to see it all in one day can be tiring.
- Underground tunnels connect different pavilions so there's no need to brave the elements between exhibitions.

Take a Break

Pop into the on-site **Le Beaux-Arts Bistro** (514-285-2000; www.mbam.qc.ca; 1384 Rue Sherbrooke Ouest; mains $13-18; 10am-4:30pm; M Guy-Concordia) in the main building so you don't miss any art.

Leave the museum for the calm of Persian teahouse Cafe Aunja (p61).

Walking Tour

Delving into Downtown

Downtown Montréal's wide boulevards, glass skyscrapers and shopping galleries give the area a decidedly North American flavor, while numerous green spaces, eye-catching heritage buildings and 19th-century churches add a more European character to the bustling city streets. This walk takes in fascinating architecture, hidden public art and some memorable vantage points for taking in Montréal's bustling commercial heart.

Walk Facts

Start Sq Dorchester; M Peel

End Musée des Beaux-Arts; M Guy-Concordia

Length 2.5km, two hours

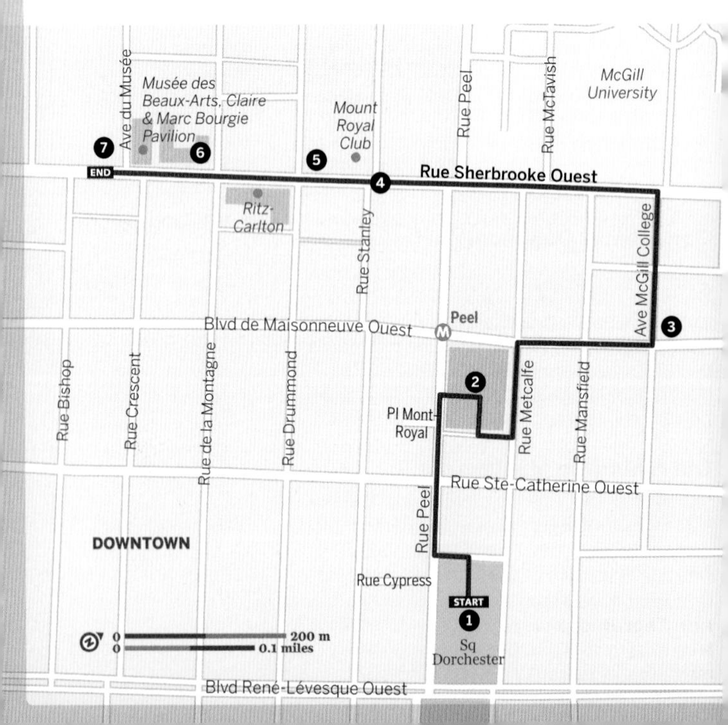

❶ Photogenic Square

Start at **Square Dorchester** (2903 Rue Peel; Ⓜ Peel). The statue to the northeast is of Lord Strathcona, a philanthropist who sponsored Canada's efforts in the South African Boer War. Wander south to see the statue of Sir Wilfrid Laurier (1841–1919), one of Canada's most respected prime ministers.

❷ Art & Shopping

Walk northwest on Rue Peel to the upscale shopping complex **Les Cours Mont-Royal** (www.lcmr.ca; 1455 Rue Peel; 10am-6pm Mon-Wed, to 9pm Thu & Fri, to 5pm Sat, noon-5pm Sun; Ⓜ Peel). The central atrium has bird sculptures with human heads by Inuit artist David Ruben Piqtoukun, and a chandelier from a Monte Carlo casino. Cut through the building and continue up Rue Metcalf.

❸ Mob Mentality

Turn right on Blvd de Maisonneuve Ouest and left on Ave McGill College. About 20m up the block on the right is the **Illuminated Crowd** (1981 Ave McGill College; 24hr; Ⓜ McGill) sculpture. Designed by Raymond Mason, it illuminates the darker side of human nature.

❹ Majestic Facades

Continue on and turn left at **Rue Sherbrooke Ouest** (p60), Montréal's most prestigious residential street in the early 20th century. It features glorious old homes, including the Mount Royal Club, once an exclusive men-only club that now opens its doors to all.

❺ Living in Grandeur

Nearby, impressive **Reid Wilson House** (1187 Rue Sherbrooke Ouest; Ⓜ Peel) is a mansion with its original carriage house in the back and an attached conservatory. Continue along Sherbrooke; you'll soon reach the Ritz-Carlton, which has a lavish afternoon tea in the Palm Court.

❻ Creative Architecture

Further along Sherbrooke, you'll pass fortress-like apartment complex **Le Château** (1321 Rue Sherbrooke Ouest; Ⓜ Guy-Concordia), with vestiges of shell fossils in the limestone. Next door there is a massive stone church with Tiffany stained-glass windows. It now houses the Bourgie Concert Hall, part of the Claire & Marc Bourgie Pavilion at the Musée des Beaux-Arts.

❼ Artful Symmetry

End your tour with a look at the neoclassical facade of the museum's **Michal & Renata Hornstein Pavilion** (p53). Each of the symmetrical ionic columns took six men three months to cut and shape with pneumatic hammers.

Parc du Mont-Royal
Redpath Cres
Ave Cedar
Ave des Pins Ouest
Parc Percy Walters
Parc Rutherford
Ave Docteur-Penfield
McGill University
4 Musée Redpath
Rue Simpson
Rue Redpath
Ave du Musée
Rue de la Montagne
Rue Drummond
Rue Peel
Rue McTavish
Rue University
Rue Sherbrooke Ouest
6
Musée McCord
2
10
Musée des Beaux-Arts de Montréal
Rue Metcalfe
Ave McGill College
Rue Victoria
Guy-Concordia
Blvd de Maisonneuve Ouest
Peel
McGill
Concordia University
16
30
Centre Infotouriste Montréal
Rue Ste-Catherine Ouest
23
DOWNTOWN
14
17
9
8
22
13
Rue Cathcart
Rue Guy
Rue Mackay
Rue Bishop
Rue Crescent
Rue Stanley
Rue Mansfield
Sq Dorchester
15
Blvd René-Lévesque Ouest
Pl du Canada
7
Cathédrale Marie-Reine-du-Monde
Rue Belmont
Gare Centrale
Ave Overdale
Ave Argyle
Lucien-L'Allier
Bell Centre
Bonaventure
Rue de la Cathédrale
Rue St-Antoine Ouest
Rue Lusignan
Rue Versailles
Rue Lucien-L'Allier
Rue Torrance
Rue Jean-d'Estrées
Rue St-Jacques
Sq Chaboillez
Pl Victor Hugo
Parc Labatt
A
B
C
D
1
2
3
4
5
6

Ave des Pins Ouest
Ave des Pins Est
Rue Guilbault
0 500 m
0 0.25 miles
Rue Prince-Arthur Ouest
Ave Lorne
Rue Aylmer
Rue Durocher
Rue Hutchison
Ave du Parc
Rue Jeanne-Mance
Rue Ste-Famille
Rue St-Urbain
Rue Clark
Blvd St-Laurent
Rue St-Dominique
Ave Coloniale
Rue de Bullion
Ave de l'Hôtel-de-Ville
Ave Laval
Rue Milton
Rue Sherbrooke Est
Rue Sherbrooke Ouest
Rue St-Norbert
Rue Evans
Rue Ontario Est
Rue Ontario Ouest
Ave du Président Kennedy
Rue City Councillors
Blvd de Maisonneuve Ouest
Blvd de Maisonneuve Est
St-Laurent
Place-des-Arts
Place des Arts
Musée d'Art Contemporain
Rue Mayor
Rue Ste-Catherine Ouest
Rue Ste-Catherine Est
Galeries d'Art Contemporain du Belgo
Rue de Bleury
Rue Charlotte
Pl de la Paix
Blvd René-Lévesque Ouest
Blvd René-Lévesque Est
Côte du Beaver Hall
Rue St-Alexandre
Rue Anderson
Rue Dowd
Rue de la Gauchetière Ouest
CHINATOWN
Place-d'Armes
Rue Ste-Élisabeth
Ave Viger Est
Ave Viger Ouest
Champ-de-Mars
Autoroute Ville-Marie
Pl Jean-Paul-Riopelle
Rue St-Antoine Ouest
Sq Victoria
Rue Square Victoria
Rue St-Pierre
Rue St-Jacques
Pl d'Armes
Rue Notre-Dame Ouest
OLD MONTRÉAL
For reviews see
Top Experiences p52
Sights p58
Eating p60
Drinking p62
Entertainment p64
Shopping p65

Sights

Place des Arts

ARTS CENTER

1 MAP P56, F3

Montréal's performing-arts center is the nexus for both artistic and cultural events. Several renowned musical companies call Place des Arts home, including **Opéra de Montréal** (514-985-2258; www.operademontreal.com; Pl des Arts; M Place-des-Arts) and the **Montréal Symphony Orchestra** (OSM; 514-840-7400; www.osm.ca; 1600 Rue St-Urbain; box office 9am-5pm Mon-Fri & 90mins before shows; M Place-des-Arts), based in the acoustically brilliant 2100-seat **Maison Symphonique**. It's also center stage for **Festival International de Jazz de Montréal** (www.montrealjazzfest.com; late Jun-early Jul). A key part of the Quartier des Spectacles, the complex embraces an outdoor plaza with fountains and an ornamental pool and is attached to the Complexe Desjardins shopping center via an underground tunnel. (box office 514-842-2112; www.placedesarts.com; 175 Rue Ste-Catherine Ouest; M Place-des-Arts)

Musée McCord

MUSEUM

2 MAP P56, D3

With hardly an inch to spare in its cramped but welcoming galleries, the McCord Museum of Canadian History houses thousands of artifacts and documents illustrating Canada's social, cultural and archaeological history from the 18th century to the present day with a small-but-excellent First Nations permanent collection displaying aboriginal dress and artifacts. (McCord Museum of Canadian History; 514-861-6701; www.mccord-museum.qc.ca; 690 Rue Sherbrooke Ouest; adult/student/child $20/14/free, special exhibitions extra $5, after 5pm Wed free; 10am-6pm Tue, Thu & Fri, to 9pm Wed, to 5pm Sat & Sun; M McGill)

Musée d'Art Contemporain

MUSEUM

3 MAP P56, F4

This showcase of modern Canadian and international art has eight different galleries divided between past greats (since 1939) and exciting current developments. A weighty collection of 7600 permanent works includes Québécois legends Jean-Paul Riopelle, Paul-Émile Borduas and Geneviève Cadieux, but also offers temporary exhibitions of the latest trends in current art from Canadian and international artists. Forms range from traditional to new media, from painting, sculpture and prints to installation art, photography and video. (514-847-6226; www.macm.org; 185 Rue Ste-Catherine Ouest; adult/child $17/6, 5-9pm Wed half price; 11am-6pm Tue, to 9pm Wed-Fri, 10am-6pm Sat & Sun; M Place-des-Arts)

Musée Redpath

MUSEUM

4 MAP P56, D2

A Victorian spirit of discovery pervades this old natural-history museum, though you won't find anything more gruesome than stuffed animals from the Laurentians hinterland. The museum houses a large variety of specimens, including a dinosaur skeleton and seashells donated from around the world. A highlight is the 3rd-floor **World Cultures Exhibits**, which includes Egyptian mummies, shrunken heads and artifacts from ancient Mediterranean, African and East Asian communities. (514-398-4086; www.mcgill.ca/redpath/; 859 Rue Sherbrooke Ouest; suggested donation adult/child $10/free; 9am-2pm Jun-Aug, 9am-5pm Mon-Fri, 11am-5pm Sat & Sun Sep-May; M McGill)

Galeries d'Art Contemporain du Belgo

ARTS CENTER

5 MAP P56, E4

More than a decade ago the Belgo building was a run-down haven for struggling artists. It has since earned a reputation as one of Montréal's most intriguing exhibition spaces with some 30 galleries and artist studios, along with dance, yoga and photography studios. Check the website for ongoing exhibitions and upcoming openings. (www.thebelgoreport.com; 372 Rue Ste-Catherine Ouest; vary; M Place-des-Arts)

Musée d'Art Contemporain

Society for Arts & Technology

Set in a sleek new-media space, **SAT** (Société des Arts Technologiques; 514-844-2033; www.sat.qc.ca; 1195 Blvd St-Laurent; M St-Laurent) hosts a range of thought-provoking exhibitions. The 360-degree Satosphere shows cutting-edge audiovisual works, while the Espace Sat stages technology-driven exhibitions and the odd theater troupe and performing artist.

Rue Sherbrooke Ouest STREET

6 MAP P56, C3

Until the 1930s the downtown stretch of Rue Sherbrooke Ouest was home to the **Golden Square Mile**, one of the richest residential neighborhoods in Canada. You'll see a few glorious old homes along this drag, including the **Reid Wilson House**, the **Louis-Joseph Forget House** (1195 Rue Sherbrooke Ouest; M Peel) and the **Mount Royal Club**. There are good interpretation panels outside them explaining their history.

Cathédrale Marie-Reine-du-Monde CHURCH

7 MAP P56, C5

The Cathedral of Mary Queen of the World is a smaller but still magnificent version of St Peter's Basilica in Rome. The architects scaled it down to a quarter of its size, mindful of the structural risks of Montréal's severe winters. This landmark was built from 1870 to 1894 as a symbol of Catholic power in the heart of Protestant Montréal. (514-866-1661; 1085 Rue de la Cathédrale; admission free; 7:30am-6:15pm; M Bonaventure)

Eating

LOV VEGETARIAN $

8 MAP P56, B4

The gold floral stylings and large marble tables of LOV might read boutique hotel, but the surprise is that this stylish vegetarian restaurant is well priced and good for both romancing somebody else, or yourself. For a starter, try the mushroom dumplings served with almond butter, or vegan poutine. Then move on to the pasta-free, cashew-cream lasagna or tofu banh-mi burgers. (514-287-1155; www.lov.com; 1232 Rue de la Montagne; mains $14-18; ; M Peel)

Foodchain VEGETARIAN $

9 MAP P56, D4

Foodchain functions like a fast-food joint, but gives a much-needed healthy option downtown with simple, mostly vegan, bowls highlighting raw vegetables. Try a simple curry, or fennel and daikon or cauliflower, mushroom and feta salads. The decoration looks lifted from a stylish kids' picture book. (www.eatfoodchain.com; 1212 Ave McGill College; mains $9-14; 10:30am-8:30pm; ; M McGill)

Cafe Aunja

CAFE $

10 MAP P56, A3

Despite the location along busy Sherbrooke, Cafe Aunja feels like an oasis from the downtown bustle. Changing artwork adorns the brick walls of this Persian teahouse, and there's a regular lineup of readings and live music. It's a mix of book-and laptop-absorbed people and quietly chatting friends enjoying sandwiches or feta, olive and egg brunches. (514-914-8337; www.aunja.com; 1448 Rue Sherbrooke Ouest; snacks $8-11; 10am-10pm; M Guy-Concordia)

Café Parvis

BISTRO $$

11 MAP P56, E3

Hidden on a quiet downtown lane, Café Parvis is set with oversized windows, hanging plants, old wooden floorboards and vintage fixtures. Once part of the fur district, this cleverly repurposed room serves up delicious pizzas ($10 at lunch; about $20 at night) in inventive combinations (such as duck, fennel and squid, ham and eggplant, or roasted vegetables with Gruyère). (514-764-3589; www.cafeparvis.com; 433 Rue Mayor; small plates $6-9; 7am-11pm Mon-Wed, to midnight Thu & Fri, 10am-midnight Sat, to 10pm Sun; ; M Place-des-Arts)

Foodlab

INTERNATIONAL $$

12 MAP P56, G4

On the upper floor of the arts center **SAT**, Foodlab is a creative culinary space where the small menu changes every two weeks, and ranges around the globe. It's a casual but handsomely designed space, where patrons perch on bar stools, sipping creative cocktails and watching fast-moving chefs in the open kitchen.There's outdoor seating in the summer and a yurt set up in the winter. (514-844-2033; http://sat.qc.ca/fr/restaurant-labo-culinaire; 3rd fl, 1201 Blvd St-Laurent; mains $14-26; 5-10pm Tue-Sat; M St-Laurent)

Le Balsam Inn

ITALIAN $$

13 MAP P56, C4

A charmer in the downtown dining scene, Le Balsam Inn serves up delectable plates of Italian fare, with standouts such as citrus-drizzled calamari, osso buco with polenta, and pasta with pancetta and parmesan. It's also a great, though noisy, spot for an evening (or afternoon) libation, with a good wine selection and well-executed cocktails. (514-507-9207; www.lebalsaminn.com; 1237 Rue Metcalfe; small plates $10-16, mains $22-26; 11:30am-11pm Tue-Fri, from 4:30pm Sat; M Peel)

Reuben's
DELI $$

14 MAP P56, C4

A classic, long-running deli, Reuben's has squishy booths and a long counter, where patrons line up for towering smoked-meat sandwiches served with big-cut fries, or pizza and pasta. Steakhouse favorites such as grilled salmon or fried chicken sit atop salad bowls – that's healthy, right? Try to avoid the busy lunch rush. (514-866-1029; http://reubensdeli.com; 1116 Rue Ste-Catherine Ouest; mains $18-28; 8am-midnight Sun-Thu, to 1:30am Fri & Sat; M Peel)

Jatoba
ASIAN $$$

15 MAP P56, D4

Celebrated chef Antonio Park is behind the menu at this artfully designed space just off Place Phillips. Park – who was born to Korean parents, grew up in South America and went to cooking school in Japan – brilliantly melds flavors from around the globe. (514-871-1184; www.jatobamontreal.com; 1184 Pl Phillips; mains $22-38; 11:30am-2:30pm & 5-10pm Mon-Fri, 5-11pm Sat; ; M McGill)

Ferreira Café
PORTUGUESE $$$

16 MAP P56, C3

This inviting restaurant serves some of Montréal's best Portuguese fare. The *cataplana* (a bouillabaisse-style seafood stew) is magnificent; tender morsels of delicious grilled fish are cooked to perfection, while meat lovers can feast on rack of lamb or spice-rubbed Angus rib-eye steak. Late diners can enjoy two-course, $30 meals from 10pm to close. (514-848-0988; www.ferreiracafe.com; 1446 Rue Peel; mains $26-49; 11:45am-3pm Mon-Fri, 5:30-11pm Mon-Wed, 5:30pm-midnight Thu-Sat, 5-10pm Sun; M Peel)

Drinking

Dominion Square Tavern
TAVERNA

17 MAP P56, C4

Once a down-and-out watering hole dating from the 1920s, this beautifully renovated tavern recalls a classic French bistro but with a long bar, English pub–style. Executive chef Éric Dupuis puts his own spin on pub grub, with mussels cooked with bacon, and smoked trout salad with curry dressing. (514-564-5056; www.tavernedominion.com; 1243 Rue Metcalfe; 11:30am-midnight Mon-Fri, 4:30pm-midnight Sat & Sun; M Peel)

Furco
COCKTAIL BAR

18 MAP P56, E3

In a previous life this stylish but industrial hideaway was a fur factory, and its raw concrete pillars, copper bar and modular light fixtures form the backdrop to a buzzing eating and drinking scene just a short stroll from Place-des-Arts. You'll find well-crafted cocktails and upmarket snacks (come for $1 oysters on

Sundays and Mondays). (514-764-3588; www.barfurco.com; 425 Rue Mayor; 4pm-3am Mon-Sat; M Place-des-Arts)

Biirū

BAR

19 MAP P56, E4

Despite the name, this colorfully designed *izakaya* doesn't serve much *biirū* (beer). It does have creative cocktails, tasty snacks and a festive environment that draws the after-work crowd. You can nibble on *gyoza* (dumplings), duck *magret* salad or mushroom *okonomiyaki* (Japanese pancake), while admiring the Hokusai-inspired mural. (514-903-1555; www.biiru.ca; 1433 Rue City Councillors; 11:30am-2:30pm Mon-Fri, 5:30-10pm Tue-Thu & Sun, 5:30-11pm Fri & Sat; M McGill)

Pub Ste-Élisabeth

PUB

20 MAP P56, H4

Tucked off a side street, this handsome little pub is frequented by many for its heavenly vine-covered courtyard and drinks menu with a great selection of beers, whiskeys and ports. It has a respectable lineup of beers on tap, including imports and microbrewery fare such as Boréale Noire and Cidre Mystique. (514-286-4302; www.ste-elisabeth.com; 1412 Rue Ste-Élisabeth; 4pm-3am; M Berri-UQAM)

Pullman

BAR

21 MAP P56, F2

This beautifully designed wine bar is a favorite haunt of the 30-something set. It's primarily

Ferreira Café

a restaurant, but the downstairs bar of this two-level space gets jammed (or *jammé*, as they say in Franglais) after work and becomes quite a pickup spot, so be prepared to engage in some flirting. Knowledgeable staff can help you choose from the sprawling wine list. (514-288-7779; www.pullman-mtl.com; 3424 Ave du Parc; 4:30pm-midnight Sun-Tue, to 1am Wed-Sat; M Place-des-Arts)

Brutopia

BREWERY

22 MAP P56, B4

This fantastic brewpub has eight varieties of suds on tap, including honey beer, nut brown and the more challenging raspberry blonde – all with ingredients from Québécois farms. The brick walls and wood paneling are conducive to chats among the student crowd. Live blues bands play nightly (from 10pm). Things pick up after the night classes from nearby Concordia get out. (514-393-9277; www.brutopia.net; 1219 Rue Crescent; 2pm-3am Sun-Wed, noon-3am Thu-Sat; M Guy-Concordia)

Upstairs

BAR

23 MAP P56, A4

This slick downtown bar hosts quality jazz and blues acts every night, featuring both local and touring talent. The walled terrace behind the bar is enchanting at sunset, and the dinner menu features inventive salads and meals such as the Cajun bacon burger. (514-931-6808; www.upstairsjazz.com; 1254 Rue Mackay; 11:30am-1am Mon-Thu, to 2am Fri, 5:30pm-2am Sat, 6:30pm-1am Sun; M Guy-Concordia)

Entertainment

Gesù

JAZZ

24 MAP P56, F4

This small live-music and events venue at the basement of a church is truly blessed with character. Its Greek-theater acoustics mean that you can see and hear well no matter which seat you're in. The religious setting has absolutely no bearing on the performances, which include everything from stand-up comedy to jazz to kids' shows, and even the Montréal Gay Men's Chorus. (514-861-4378; www.legesu.com; 1200 Rue de Bleury; shows $18-57; box office noon-6:30pm Tue-Sat)

L'Astral

LIVE MUSIC

25 MAP P56, F4

The century-old Blumenthal Building is a polished venue of Montréal's jazz fest as part of the Quartier des Spectacles. With more than 300 seats and standing room for 600, L'Astral nestles in the Maison du Festival Rio Tinto Alcan, which also houses **Le Balmoral**, a jazz club and bistro with a patio on the ground floor. (www.sallelastral.com; 305 Rue Ste-Catherine Ouest; M Place-des-Arts)

Monument National

PERFORMING ARTS

26 MAP P56, G4

Québec's oldest theater still in use, the grand Monument National opened in 1893, and has been showing a wide range of cultural fare ever since. Shows here run the gamut from Molière to Sam Shepard, with acting, directing and technical production performed by graduating students of the National Theatre School. (514-871-2224; www.monumentnational.com; 1182 Blvd St-Laurent; M St-Laurent)

Foufounes Électriques

LIVE MUSIC

27 MAP P56, H4

A one-time bastion of the alternafreak, this cavernous quintessential punk venue still stages some wild music nights (retro Tuesdays, hip-hop Thursdays, rockabilly/metal/punk Saturdays), plus the odd one-off (a night of prowrestling or an indoor skateboarding contest). The graffiti-covered walls and industrial charm should tip you off that 'Electric Buttocks' isn't exactly a mainstream kinda place. (514-844-5539; www.foufouneselectriques.com; 87 Rue Ste-Catherine Est; cover $4-6; 4pm-3am; M St-Laurent)

Agora de la Danse

DANCE

28 MAP P56, F4

One of Montréal's most important names in the contemporary-dance world, Agora de la Danse explores modern and experimental forms, staging both homegrown troupes and performers from around the globe. It's within the Wilder building. (514-525-1500; http://agoradanse.com; 1435 Rue de Bleury; tickets around $30; box office noon-5pm; M Place-des-Arts)

Shopping

Eva B

VINTAGE

29 MAP P56, G3

Stepping into this graffiti-smeared building on St-Laurent is like entering a theater's backstage, with a riot of vintage coats, bowling shirts, cowboy boots, leather jackets, wigs, and denim of all shapes and sizes. There's lots of junk, but prices are low, and you can probably unearth a few treasures if you have the time. (514-849-8246; www.eva-b.ca; 2015 Blvd St-Laurent; 11am-7pm Mon-Sat, noon-6pm Sun; M St-Laurent)

Holt Renfrew Ogilvy

CLOTHING

30 MAP P56, B4

Founded in 1866 as Canada's first department store, Ogilvy has transformed itself into a collection of high-profile boutiques. The store's front window displays mechanical toys that are a Montréal fixture at Christmas. (www.holtrenfrew.com/en/the-new-holt-renfrew-ogilvy; 1307 Rue Ste-Catherine Ouest; 10am-6pm Mon-Wed, to 9pm Thu & Fri, 9:30am-6:30pm Sat, 11am-6pm Sun; M Peel)

STARBUCKS COFFEE
BBQ
Ristorante
STARBUCKS COFFEE

Explore

Rue St-Denis & the Village

Rue St-Denis in the Quartier Latin is a gateway to theaters, lively cafes and low-key bars packed with students from the French-speaking Université du Québec à Montréal. Closed shop fronts in recent years have created a treasure hunt for gems amongst the grunge. Continue west to reach the Village, a major icon for gay travelers. Shops, restaurants and bars proudly fly the rainbow colors here, and the nightlife and cafe scene rarely slows down.

The Short List

- ***Rue St-Denis (p68)*** *Sipping un café, beer or whiskey and soaking up the ever-changing atmosphere on this colorful street.*
- ***Écomusée du Fier Monde (p71)*** *Stepping back in time to the 1920s for a glimpse of life in working-class Montréal.*
- ***Cabaret Mado (p73)*** *Sashaying from the sidelines at a cabaret drag show in the Village.*

Getting There & Around

M Key stops are Berri-UQAM, Beaudry and Papineau.

Bus 24 runs along Rue Sherbrooke, the 30 along Rue St-Denis and Rue Berri, and the 15 along Rue Ste-Catherine.

It's relatively easy to reach Rue St-Denis from either Downtown or Plateau Mont-Royal, and you can also stroll along Rue Ste-Catherine to the Village.

Rue St-Denis Map on p70

Rue St-Denis (p68) IAN DAGNALL/ALAMY STOCK PHOTO ©

Top Experience

Watch the World Go By on Rue St-Denis

This street captures the heart of francophone Montréal. A carnivalesque collection of restaurants, brasseries, cafes and arts venues coalesce in four blocks along Rue St-Denis below Rue Sherbrooke. You'll find students from nearby Université du Québec à Montréal (UQAM) grabbing a pint after protesting tuition hikes, or big-name US comics doing stand-up at Théâtre St-Denis.

MAP P70, B2

M Berri-UQAM

Eat, Drink & Be Merry

The quarter is a hotbed of activity, especially during summer festivals, when energy spills from the streets 24 hours a day. The terraced cafes and restaurants of Rue St-Denis are great spots to watch the world go by, over coffee, croissants or even a bowl of borscht. Popular with students at UQAM, who number in the tens of thousands, the street is all about budget dining, inexpensive bistro fare and meals in a hurry.

There are also abundant bars nearby, making for an easy transition from dinner to nighttime amusement. Rue St-Denis is one of the few streets to cross the entire island of Montréal and the bars become a little more upmarket-cool as you head west toward Mont-Royal.

The Village

Rue St-Denis is an entry of sorts to the Village, one of the largest gay communities in North America. Packed with eclectic eateries, shops and outrageous nightspots, Rue Ste-Catherine is the Village's main thoroughfare; it closes to traffic periodically in the summer.

Architectural Gems

In the 19th century, the neighborhood was an exclusive residential area for wealthy francophones. Although many original buildings burned in the great fire of 1852, there are a number of Victorian and art-nouveau gems hidden on the tree-lined streets. (pictured)

Street Art

The street and its surrounds (between Rue St-Denis and south to Blvd St-Laurent) are dotted with street art, including spectacular murals that are social-media friendly. Pictured is a wall mural at 1755 Rue St-Denis by Carlito Dalceggio.

★ Top Tips

- Rue St-Denis might have lost many stalwart boutique shops and fine restaurants, but come here with a budget-minded attitude and you will have a good time.
- If you love walking, Rue St-Denis is a convenient rest stop between Chinatown and the Village.
- Head to the backstreets off Rue St-Denis for hidden cafes.

✕ Take a Break

Grab a pint or coffee and relax in the garden with the students at Le Saint Sulpice (p72).

Try a Haitian snack or meal at Agrikol (p72).

For reviews see

Top Experiences	p68
Sights	p71
Eating	p72
Drinking	p72
Entertainment	p73
Shopping	p73

A
B
C
D
E
F
1
2
3
4
0 200 m
0 0.1 miles
Rue Sherbrooke Est
QUARTIER LATIN
Rue Ontario Est
Rue St-Denis
2 Écomusée du Fier Monde
3
4
5
6
7
8
9
10
11
Ave Lalonde
Rue La Fontaine
Rue Robin
Rue Logan
THE VILLAGE
Blvd St-Laurent
Rue St-Dominique
Ave de l'Hôtel-de-Ville
Rue Émery
Ave Savoie
Rue Berri
Rue St-Hubert
Rue St-Christophe
Rue St-André
Rue Labrecque
Rue St-Timothée
Rue Amherst
Rue Wolfe
Rue Montcalm
Rue Beaudry
Rue Mercure
Rue de la Visitation
Rue Panet
Rue Plessis
Rue Alexandre-de-Sève
Rue de Champlain
St-Laurent
Berri-UQAM
Gare d'Autocars de Montréal
Blvd de Maisonneuve Est
Rue Martineau
Rue de Boisbriand
Université du Québec à Montréal
Pl Émilie-Gamelin
Beaudry
Rue Ste-Catherine Est
Rue de Bullion
Rue Ste-Élisabeth
Rue Sanguinet
Rue Labelle
Rue Ste-Rose
Rue Dalcourt
Rue Charlotte
Pl de la Paix
Blvd René-Lévesque Est
Église St-Pierre-Apôtre 1

Sights

Église St-Pierre-Apôtre CHURCH

1 MAP P70, E4

Located in the Village, this neoclassical church from 1853 has fine decorations – flying buttresses, stained glass, statues in Italian marble – but nowadays is more known for its gay-friendly Sunday services. It houses the Chapel of Hope, consecrated in 1997, the first chapel in the world dedicated to the memory of victims of AIDS. The Church of St Peter the Apostle belonged to the monastery of the Oblate fathers who settled in Montréal in the mid-19th century. (514-524-3791; www.saintpierreapotre.ca; 1201 Rue de la Visitation; noon-4pm Mon-Fri, to 5:15 Sat, 10am-4pm Su; M Beaudry)

Écomusée du Fier Monde MUSEUM

2 MAP P70, D1

This striking ex-bathhouse explores the history of Centre-Sud, an industrial district in Montréal until the 1950s and now part of the Village. The museum's permanent exhibition, *Triumphs and Tragedies of a Working-Class Neighborhood*, puts faces on the industrial era through a series of photos and multimedia displays. The 1927 building is the former Bain Généreux, an art-deco public bathhouse modeled on one in Paris. (514-528-8444; http://ecomusee.qc.ca; 2050 Rue Amherst; adult/child $8/6, $2 discount with STM tickets; 11am-8pm Wed, 9:30am-4pm Thu & Fri, 10:30am-5pm Sat & Sun; M Berri-UQAM)

Église St-Pierre-Apôtre

Eating

Agrikol

CARIBBEAN **$$**

3 MAP P70, D1

This Haitian restaurant was originally opened by musicians of Arcade Fire. A casual but elevated diner vibe with hip staff serving dishes like small plates of plantains and *chiktay* (smoked herring), and the namesake rum drink. (514-903-6707; www.agrikol.ca; 1844 Rue Amherst; mains $12-25; 5pm-midnight, also 11am-3pm Sun; ; M Beaudry)

O'Thym

FRENCH **$$**

4 MAP P70, D3

O'Thym buzzes with foodies from all over town. It features an elegant but understated dining room, and beautifully presented plates such as Eastern Township rabbit with mustard and a fusion kimchi-sumac duck breast. Bring your own wine. (514-525-3443; www.othym.com; 1112 Blvd de Maisonneuve Est; mains brunch $16-24, dinner $23-37; 10am-2pm Sat & Sun, 5:30-10pm nightly; M Beaudry)

Saloon

BISTRO **$$**

5 MAP P70, E3

With nearly 20 years under its belt, this gay bar-bistro has earned a spot in Village hearts for its chilled atmosphere, live DJs, patio seating, cocktails and wide-ranging menu, including salmon bowls, steaks, burgers, and some good vegetarian options. A stylish preclub stop or a good-value spot for set lunches (from $12.75). (514-522-1333; www.lesaloon.ca; 1333 Rue Ste-Catherine Est; mains $16-28; 11:30am-2pm & 5-10pm Mon-Wed, 11:30am-11pm Thu-Fri, 10am-11pm Sat & Sun; M Beaudry)

Drinking

Le Cheval Blanc

MICROBREWERY

6 MAP P70, C1

An icon of Montréal's brewery scene, Le Cheval Blanc has about 10 drafts on hand, all brewed in house, as well as some Belgian options by the bottle. It's a lively, easygoing place with a friendly all-ages crowd. (514-522-0211; http://lechevalblanc.ca; 809 Rue Ontario Est; 3pm-3am; M Sherbrooke)

Le Saint Sulpice

PUB

7 MAP P70, B2

This student evergreen is spread over four levels in an old Victorian stone house – a cafe, several terraces, a disco, karaoke and a sprawling back garden. The music changes with the DJ's mood, from hip-hop and ambient to rock and jazz. (514-844-9458; www.lesaintsulpice.ca; 1680 Rue St-Denis; 3:30pm-3:30am Tue-Sun; M Berri-UQAM)

Entertainment

Le 4e Mur
LIVE MUSIC

8 MAP P70, B1

This bar is literally behind an unmarked door – look for a big intimidating bouncer. Follow on, into a basement bar of low lighting and wicker chairs where the cocktails are expertly mixed, live music pops off regularly, and burlesque is a regular fixture. (http://le4emur.com; 2021 Rue St-Denis; 5pm-3am, from 7pm Sun; M Sherbrooke)

Cabaret Mado
CABARET

9 MAP P70, D3

Mado is a flamboyant celebrity who has been featured in *Fugues*. Her cabaret is a local institution, with drag shows featuring an assortment of hilariously sarcastic performers in eye-popping costumes. Shows take place Tuesday, Thursday and weekend nights; check the website for details. (514-525-7566; www.mado.qc.ca; 1115 Rue Ste-Catherine Est; tickets $5-15; 4pm-3am Tue-Sun; M Beaudry)

Shopping

Camellia Sinensis
FOOD & DRINKS

10 MAP P70, B2

Right in front of the Cinéma Quartier Latin, this tea shop has over 200 varieties of tea from China, Japan, India and elsewhere in Asia, plus quality teapots, tea accessories, books, and workshops such as pairing tea with chocolate. Taste teas and desserts in the salon next door, featuring brews from recent staff travels. (www.camellia-sinensis.com; 351 Rue Émery; noon-10pm Mon-Thu, to 11pm Sat, to 9pm Sun; M Berri-UQAM)

Priape
ADULT

11 MAP P70, E3

Montréal's biggest gay sex store is well plugged into mainstream erotic wares (DVDs, mags and books), and also has high-quality clothing with a titillating edge – shrink-wrapped jeans, but also a vast choice of black leather gear in the basement. (514-521-8451; www.priape.com; 1311 Rue Ste-Catherine Est; 10am-8pm Mon, to 9pm Tue-Thu, to 10pm Fri & Sat, noon-8pm; M Beaudry)

4410

Plateau Mont-Royal

This cool neighborhood houses a wealth of sidewalk cafes, excellent restaurants, and bars and boutiques. For many Montréalers and visitors alike, exploring the Plateau is the essence of experiencing Montréal. The former immigrant neighborhood with its colorful characters was immortalized by francophone playwright Michel Tremblay. The Plateau is also handily located next to the city's beloved 'mountain,' Mont-Royal.

The Short List

- ***Boulevard St-Laurent (p80)*** *Exploring the old-world groceries that rub shoulders with stylish drinking dens.*
- ***Parc La Fontaine (p80)*** *Relaxing in summer and ice skating in winter in the broad expanse.*

Getting There & Around

M Metro stations of Sherbrooke, Mont-Royal and Laurier.

The 55 runs along Blvd St-Laurent; bus 30 coasts along Rue St-Denis; bus 80 travels Ave du Parc; bus 11 climbs up to Parc du Mont-Royal from Ave du Mont-Royal.

You can rent a Bixi bike to reach much of Plateau Mont-Royal.

Plateau Mont-Royal Map on p78

Plateau Mont-Royal RICHARD CAVALLERI/SHUTTERSTOCK ©

Walking Tour

Strolling the Plateau

Originally a working-class district, the Plateau changed its stripes in the 1960s and '70s when writers, singers and other creative folk moved in. Although gentrification has arrived, the neighborhood still has a bohemian edge. It's also one of Montréal's most emblematic neighborhoods, with streetscapes set with winding staircases, ornate wrought-iron balconies and pointy Victorian roofs.

Walk Facts

Start Carré St-Louis; M Sherbrooke

End Rue Cherrier; M Sherbrooke

Length 3km; one to two hours

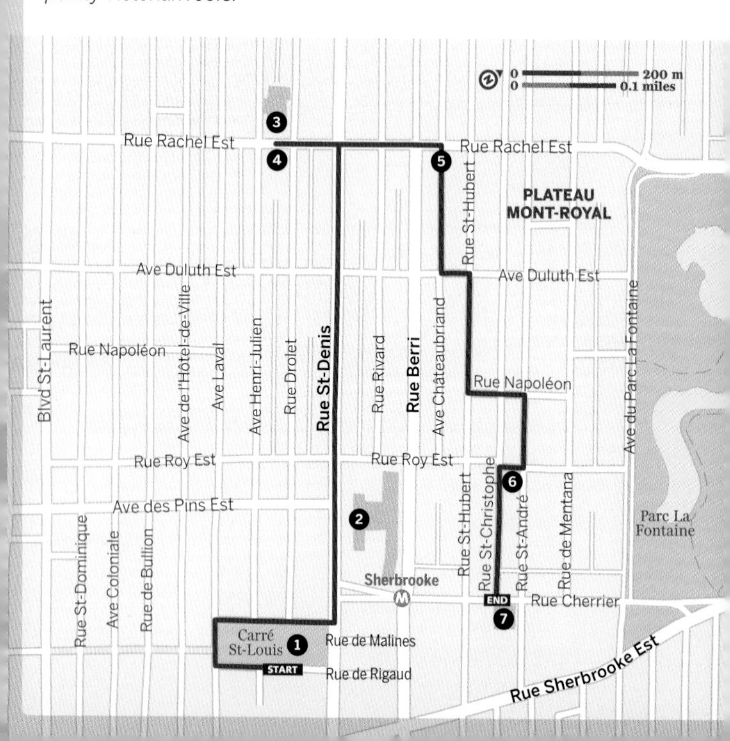

❶ Leafy Oasis

Start at the **Carré St-Louis**, a pleasant, green, shady oasis with a splashing fountain that's a popular spot for lazing and people-watching. It's surrounded by beautiful old houses built for wealthy French residents in the 19th century.

❷ St-Denis Landmark

Walk around the park (stopping for a coffee at the summertime cafe near Ave Laval), then turn left up Rue St-Denis. On your right you'll pass the majestic buildings of the former Institut des Sourdes-Muettes – note the little silver cupola. The institute was dedicated to the education of deaf, and later also blind, students, and is now known as the Institut Raymond-Dewar.

❸ Baroque Finery

Continue up Rue St-Denis and turn left onto Rue Rachel Est. You'll see the baroque **Église St-Jean-Baptiste** (http://eglisesjb.com; 4237 Ave Henri-Julien; ⌚4-6pm Mon-Thu, 4:30-6:30pm Sat, 9:30-11am & 4:30-6:30pm Sun; Ⓜ Mont-Royal), its enormous interior decorated with gilded wood and pink marble. The acoustics are excellent, making it popular for concerts.

❹ Park Views

Exiting the church, look right to see the winged angel on the imposing Sir George-Étienne Cartier monument, way down the end of the street at the leafy base of Mont-Royal. Directly opposite the church stands Les Cours Rachel, once a boarding school but now converted into condos.

❺ Rejuvenated Streets

Walk northeast along Rue Rachel Est and turn right onto Ave Châteaubriand. A rundown street in the 1970s, today this narrow lane has been spruced up with blue, green and turquoise paint and potted plants hanging outside the windows. Here you'll spot another of this town's signature objects: the external staircase.

❻ Global Art

Zigzag down to the corner of Rues Roy and St-André. You'll find Place Roy, a tiny leafy square with an art installation by sculptor Michel Goulet. Draw your own conclusions about the meaning of the world map juxtaposed with a random arrangement of chairs, some knocked to the ground.

❼ Dance Center

Walk one block to the right along Rue Roy and turn left down Rue St-Christophe. Continue to Rue Cherrier to see a lovely 1918 Italian Renaissance building. It once housed the Palestre Nationale but now belongs to UQAM and Agora de la Danse, a key name in Montréal's contemporary dance scene.

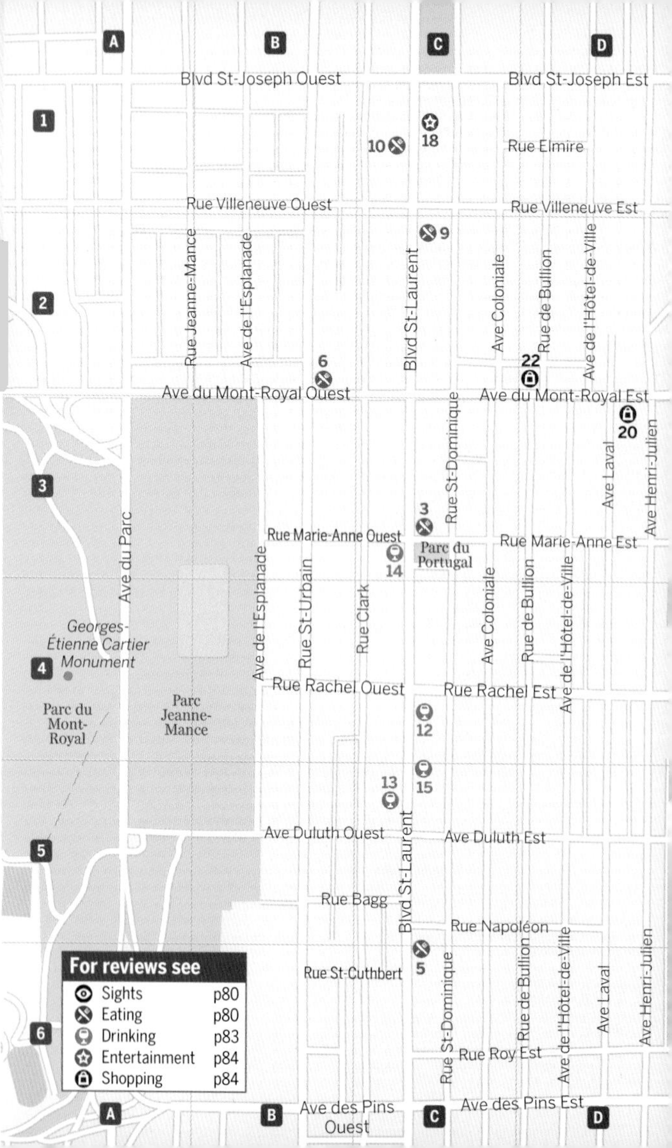

A B C D

1 2 3 4 5 6

Blvd St-Joseph Ouest
Blvd St-Joseph Est
Rue Elmire
Rue Villeneuve Ouest
Rue Villeneuve Est
Rue Jeanne-Mance
Ave de l'Esplanade
Blvd St-Laurent
Ave Coloniale
Rue de Bullion
Ave de l'Hôtel-de-Ville
Ave du Mont-Royal Ouest
Ave du Mont-Royal Est
Rue St-Dominique
Ave Laval
Ave Henri-Julien
Rue Marie-Anne Ouest
Rue Marie-Anne Est
Parc du Portugal
Ave du Parc
Rue St-Urbain
Rue Clark
Georges-Étienne Cartier Monument
Parc du Mont-Royal
Parc Jeanne-Mance
Rue Rachel Ouest
Rue Rachel Est
Ave Duluth Ouest
Ave Duluth Est
Rue Bagg
Rue Napoléon
Rue St-Cuthbert
Rue Roy Est
Ave des Pins Ouest
Ave des Pins Est

3 5 6 9 10 12 13 14 15 18 20 22

For reviews see

Sights	p80
Eating	p80
Drinking	p83
Entertainment	p84
Shopping	p84

Blvd St-Joseph Est
400 m
0.2 miles
Laurier
Rue Gilford
Rue Rivard
Rue Berri
Rue Pontiac
Rue Resther
Rue St-Hubert
Rue de Mentana
Rue Boyer
Ave Christophe Colomb
Rue de la Roche
Rue de Brébeuf
Rue Chambord
Rue de Lanaudière
Rue de Bienville
Mont-Royal
Rue Généreux
Ave du Mont-Royal Est
Avenue du Mont-Royal
Rue St-Denis
Rue Marie-Anne Est
Rue St-Hubert
Rue St-Christophe
Rue St-André
PLATEAU MONT-ROYAL
Ave Bureau
Rue Rachel Est
Ave Calixa Lavallée
Parc La Fontaine
Ave du Parc La Fontaine
Ave Duluth Est
Rue Napoléon
Rue Roy Est
Ave Châteaubriand
Rue Berri
Rue Rivard
Rue St-Denis
Rue de Mentana
1
2
4
7
8
11
16
17
19
21
E
F
G
H

Sights

Parc La Fontaine

PARK

1 MAP P78, H5

At 34 hectares, this great verdant municipal park is the city's third largest, after **Parc du Mont-Royal** (p86) and Parc Maisonneuve. In the warmer months weary urbanites flock to leafy La Fontaine to enjoy the walking and bicycle paths, the attractive ponds and the general air of relaxation that pervades the park. There's also a chalet where you can grab a bite or a drink, **Espace La Fontaine** (514-280-2525; https://espacelafontaine.com; 3933 Ave du Parc La Fontaine; mains $10-16; 11am-7pm Wed-Fri, 10am-5pm Sat & Sun; ; ; M Sherbrooke). (6am-midnight; ; ; M Sherbrooke)

Exploring the Main

Boulevard St-Laurent, (M St-Laurent then bus 55) once known as 'the Main', is the dividing line between the city's east and west. It has always been a focus of action, a gathering place for people of many languages and backgrounds. In 1996 it was declared a national historic site for its role as ground zero for so many Canadian immigrants and future Montréalers. The label 'the Main' has stuck in the local lingo since the 19th century. Today it's a gateway into the Plateau and a fascinating street to explore.

Avenue du Mont-Royal

AREA

2 MAP P78, E2

Old-fashioned five-and-dime stores rub shoulders with a wide array of trendy cafes and fashion boutiques on Ave du Mont-Royal. The nightlife here has surged to the point that it rivals Blvd St-Laurent, with bars and nightclubs ranging from the sedate to uproarious. Intimate shops, secondhand stores and ultramodern boutiques offer eye-catching apparel. (; M Mont-Royal)

Eating

Omnivore

MEDITERRANEAN $

3 MAP P78, C3

Amid rustic wood tables and potted plants, the friendly staff at little Omnivore whip up delicious Middle-Eastern mezze plates of hummus, tabbouleh, baba ghanoush, meat skewers and other Lebanese classics. There are also grilled pita sandwiches. Everything is fresh, generous and delicious and can be made vegetarian. (www.omnivoregrill.com; 4351 Blvd St-Laurent; mains $6-14; noon-9pm; ; M Mont-Royal)

La Banquise

QUÉBÉCOIS $

4 MAP P78, G4

A Montréal legend since 1968, La Banquise is probably the best place in town to sample poutine. More than 30 varieties are available, including a vegan poutine, the boogalou (with pulled pork) and straight-up classic poutine. There's an outdoor terrace, a full breakfast menu and a selection of microbrews, plus the kitchen never closes. Expect long lines on weekends. (514-525-2415; www.labanquise.com; 994 Rue Rachel Est; mains $8-15; 24hr; ; M Mont-Royal)

Schwartz's

SANDWICHES $

Reuben Schwartz opened this iconic Jewish deli in 1928 and it's been going strong ever since. Schwartz's meat goes through a 14-day regime of curing and smoking before landing on your plate after a final three-hour steam. Considered the best smoked meat in Montréal, whether it's brisket, duck, chicken or

Tam-Tam Jam Concerts

Huge crowds of alternative free spirits gather every Sunday afternoon in summer for the legendary 'tam-tam' concerts at the edge of Parc du Mont-Royal, when the pounding rhythms and whirling dancers seem to put everyone in a trance. The action takes place at the **Georges-Étienne Cartier monument** (Map p78, A4; http://ville.montreal.qc.ca; Ave du Parc; M Mont-Royal, then bus 97) opposite Parc Jeanne-Mance, at the corner of Ave du Parc and Ave Duluth.

Schwartz's

turkey, all piled high on sourdough rye bread. (☎514-842-4813; www.schwartzsdeli.com; 3895 Blvd St-Laurent; sandwiches $10.50, mains $13-26; ⏰8am-12:30am Sun-Thu, to 1:30am Fri & Sat; M Sherbrooke)

Beauty's

DINER $

6 MAP P78, B2

This sleek, retro '50s diner serves what some consider Montréal's best breakfast – all day long. Ask for 'the Special' – a toasted bagel with lox, cream cheese, tomato and onion. Lineups on Saturday and Sunday mornings can run up to 40 minutes long, even in winter (arrive before 10am). (☎514-849-8883; http://beautys.ca; 93 Ave du Mont-Royal Ouest; breakfasts $8.50-14; ⏰7am-3pm Mon-Fri, 8am to 4pm Sat & Sun; M Mont-Royal)

L'Express

FRENCH $$

7 MAP P78, E6

L'Express has all the hallmarks of a Parisian bistro – black-and-white checkered floor, art-deco globe lights, papered tables and mirrored walls. High-end bistro fare completes the picture, with excellent dishes such as grilled salmon, bone marrow with sea salt, roast duck with salad and beef tartare. The waiters can advise on the extensive wine list. Reservations are essential. (☎514-845-5333; www.restaurantlexpress.com; 3927 Rue St-Denis; mains $19-29; ⏰8am-2am Mon-Fri, from 10am Sat & Sun; M Sherbrooke)

L'Gros Luxe

BISTRO $$

8 MAP P78, E5

With classy vintage decor, booths or tables and inexpensive comfort fare, L'Gros Luxe has obvious appeal. The small dining room is always packed with young Plateau residents who come for pork tacos, veggie burgers, and fish and chips. Plates are small, but nothing costs more than $10, and there's an extensive drinks menu (with much higher prices than the food). (☎514-447-2227; www.lgrosluxe.com; 451 Ave Duluth Est; small plates $5-10; ⏰5-11:30pm Mon-Fri, from 11am Sat & Sun; ; M Sherbrooke)

Robin des Bois

FUSION $$

9 MAP P78, C2

Montréal's own 'Robin Hood,' restaurateur Judy Servay donates all profits and tips from this reliable favorite to local charities. The relaxed, spacious diner vibe and varied menu is inviting to all, solo or in groups. Customisable dishes include brown rice, mashed potato, noodles or soup topped with grilled salmon or vegan tempeh. Sandwiches and salads keep everybody happy. (☎514-288-1010; www.robindesbois.ca; 4653 Blvd St-Laurent; mains $15-25; ⏰11:30am-10pm Mon-Sat; ; M St-Laurent, then bus 55)

La Sala Rosa

SPANISH $$

10 MAP P78, C1

A festive, local and often Spanish-speaking crowd comes to this little

Iberian gem. La Sala Rosa is best known for its five tasty varieties of paella (including vegetarian) as well as numerous tapas dishes and a changing lineup of Spanish specials. On Thursday nights (from 8:45pm) there's a live flamenco show and the place gets packed. (514-844-4227; www.facebook.com/lasalarosa; 4848 Blvd St-Laurent; mains $13-17; 5-11pm Tue & Wed, to 2am Thu-Sat, to 10pm Sun; ; M Laurier)

Au Pied de Cochon QUÉBÉCOIS $$$

11 MAP P78, F5

One of Montréal's most respected restaurants features extravagant pork, duck and steak dishes, along with its signature foie gras plates. Irreverent, award-winning chef Martin Picard takes simple ingredients and transforms them into works of art. Dishes are rich and portions are large, so bring an appetite. Reservations are essential. (514-281-1114; www.aupieddecochon.ca; 536 Ave Duluth Est; mains $28-48; 5pm-midnight Wed-Sun; M Mont-Royal)

Drinking

Big in Japan COCKTAIL BAR

12 MAP P78, C4

Completely concealed from the street, Big in Japan always amazes first-timers. There you are walking along bustling St-Laurent, you find the unmarked door (looking for its small window) by the address, walk down a rather unpromising corridor and emerge into a room lit with a thousand candles (or so it seems). Everything is Japanese-inspired – cocktails, whiskey, beer and bar food. (438-380-5658; 4175 Blvd St-Laurent; 5pm-3am; M St-Laurent, then bus 55)

Barfly BAR

13  MAP P78, C5

Cheap, gritty, loud, fun and a little bit out of control – just the way we like our dive bars. Live bluegrass and rockabilly bands and bedraggled hipsters hold court alongside aging rockers at this St-Laurent hole-in-the-wall. (514-284-6665; www.facebook.com/BarflyMtl; 4062 Blvd St-Laurent; 4pm-3am; M St-Laurent, then bus 55)

Le Darling COCKTAIL BAR

14 MAP P78, C3

A mix of cafe, cocktail bar and bistro, Le Darling is a one-stop spot for top-notch drinks and bistro-quality eats. Straddling a corner on Blvd St-Laurent, just a few blocks from Mont-Royal, this vibrant hybrid has lush tropical plants hanging from the ceiling and a seemingly endless collage of vintage decor. Come day or night. (www.facebook.com/RestoBarDarling; 4328 Blvd St-Laurent; 8am-3am; M Laurier)

Majestique BAR

15  MAP P78, C5

The Majestique manages to be both kitschy and classy at the same time, with wood-paneled walls, warm lighting and a buck's head presiding over the tables. The bartenders whip up some beautiful concoctions here, and the food menu is equally creative: try the *bourgots* (snails), the *tartare de cheval* (raw horse meat) or, for something simple, the *huîtres* (oysters) or *frites* (fries). (514-439-1850; www.restobarmajestique.com; 4105 Blvd St-Laurent; 4pm-3am daily, also 11am-3pm Sun; M St-Laurent, then bus 55)

Pub Pit Caribou MICROBREWERY

16 MAP P78, G4

There are some awesome microbreweries in this province, and Pit Caribou is one of the greats. It has an outpost here in Montréal that serves its full line of hearty, sudsy goodness, often accompanied by live music. (514-522-9773; www.pitcaribou.com; 951 Rue Rachel Est; 2pm-1am Sun-Wed, to 3am Thu-Sat; M Mont-Royal)

Bily Kun BAR

17 MAP P78, E3

One of the pioneers of 'tavern chic,' Bily Kun is a favorite local hangout for a chilled evening among friends. First-time visitors usually gawp at the ostrich heads that overlook the bar but soon settle into the music groove of live jazz (from 6pm to 8pm) and DJs (10pm onward). Absinthe cocktails, herbaceous liqueurs and organic beers rule. (514-845-5392; www.bilykun.com; 354 Ave du Mont-Royal Est; 3pm-3am; M Mont-Royal)

Entertainment

Casa del Popolo LIVE MUSIC

18 MAP P78, C1

One of Montréal's most charming live venues, the 'House of the People' has talented DJs and is a venue for art-house films and spoken-word performances. It is also known for its vegetarian sandwiches and salads and is associated with the tapas bar La Sala Rosa (p82) and its concert venue La Sala Rossa. (514-284-0122; www.casadelpopolo.com; 4873 Blvd St-Laurent; $5-20; noon-3am; M Laurier)

Dièse Onze LIVE MUSIC

19 MAP P78, E4

This downstairs jazz club has just the right vibe – with an intimate small stage so you can get close to the musicians. There are shows most nights, with an eclectic lineup of artists. You can have a bite while the band plays, with good tapas options as well as a few heartier mains (goat's-cheese burger, mushroom risotto). Call for reservations. (514-223-3543; www.dieseonze.com; 4115 Rue St-Denis; $10; 6pm-late; M Mont-Royal)

Shopping

Le Port de Tête BOOKS

20 MAP P78, D3

This is a wonderfully curated bookstore that often

HEMIS/ALAMY STOCK PHOTO ©

Bily Kun

showcases up-and-coming work from dynamic small publishers. The French and English selection is eclectic as hell: thousands of philosophy titles share space with plays, poetry, graphic novels and kids' books. Nonfiction is across the street. (☎514-678-9566; www.leportdetete.com; 262 Ave du Mont-Royal Est; ⏲10am-10pm Mon-Sat, to 8pm Sun; Ⓜ Mont-Royal)

Aux 33 Tours — MUSIC

21 MAP P78, H2

Hands down, Aux 33 Tours is the best record shop in the city. You'll find a staggering selection of new and used vinyl covering every genre, and there's also a decent selection of CDs. The staff are knowledgeable, the bins are well organized and the rare finds are easy to unearth. You'll find loads of albums not sold elsewhere. (☎514-524-7397; 1373 Ave du Mont-Royal Est; ⏲10am-7pm Mon-Wed, to 9pm Thu & Fri, to 6pm Sat & Sun; Ⓜ Mont-Royal, then bus 97)

Artpop — ARTS & CRAFTS

22 MAP P78, D2

Though tiny in size, Artpop is full of unique Montréal-themed gift ideas. You'll find graphic T-shirts, bags, pillowcases, iPhone covers, postcards and prints with iconic city signage (Farine Five Roses, the big Orange Julep). Other standouts include pendants, earrings and dolls by local designers. (☎514-843-3443; 129 Ave du Mont-Royal Est; ⏲10am-7pm Mon-Wed & Sat, to 9pm Thu & Fri, 11am-7pm Sun; Ⓜ Mont-Royal)

Walking Tour

Montréal's Favorite Mountain

The charming, leafy expanse of Parc du Mont-Royal is charged for a wide range of outdoor activities. The wooded slopes and grassy meadows have stunning views that make it all the more popular for walking, picnicking and other outdoor activities. The park was laid out by Frederick Law Olmsted, the architect of New York's Central Park.

Walk Facts

Start Ave des Pins Ouest; 2

End Lac aux Castors; 11

Length 6km; two hours

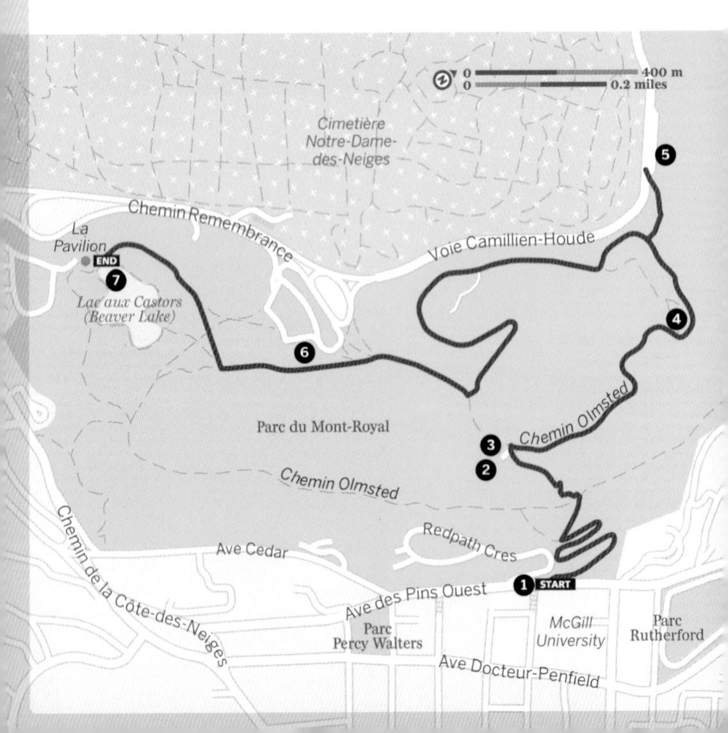

❶ Stairway to Heaven

You will find the starting point for this walk on Ave de Pins Ouest at the staircase into Parc du Mont-Royal (☎514-843-8240; www.lemontroyal.qc.ca; 1260 Chemin Remembrance; admission free; 👪; MMont-Royal, then bus 11) near the corner with Rue Peel. Be forewarned: it's a fairly steep 10- to 15-minute climb that alternates between steps and inclined, unpaved trail.

❷ Grand Views

When you reach the large path, turn right and you'll soon see yet more stairs heading up to the **Belvédère Kondiaronk lookout** (☎514-872-3911; www.lemontroyal.qc.ca; 1196 Voie Camillien-Houde; admission free; ⏰6am-midnight; MMont-Royal, then 🚌11). The wind-whipped overlook offers some absolutely stunning panoramic views of the downtown area and even beyond to the Biosphère on Parc Jean-Drapeau.

❸ The Chalet

A few paces from the lookout is the **Chalet du Mont-Royal** (☎514-843-8240; www.lemontroyal.qc.ca; 1196 Voie Camillien-Houde; admission free; ⏰10am-5pm Mon-Thu, to 8pm Fri-Sun; MMont-Royal, then 🚌 11), where you will find paintings of some key scenes from local history (and a flickering fire in winter). This is a good place to take a brisk cafe and bathroom break.

❹ Spiritual Summit

From the chalet, walk north along the trail named Chemin Olmsted about 600m to the **Croix du Mont-Royal** (MMont-Royal, then 🚌 11). This is the spot where the city's founder Maisonneuve once planted a cross in thanksgiving to the Virgin Mary for saving the city from a flood.

❺ Romantic Lookout

Further along you can descend a set of stairs to reach the scenic lookout of **Belvédère Camillien-Houde** (Voie Camillien-Houde; MMont-Royal, then bus 11), one of the most romantic views in the city.

❻ Park Exhibitions

Returning to the path, head south toward **Maison Smith** (http://ville.montreal.qc.ca; 1260 Chemin Remembrance; ⏰9am-5pm; 🚌11), an 1858 building that houses a permanent exhibition on the history and ongoing conservation of Mont-Royal. A visitor center doles out information on the park if you fancy learning more, and the on-site cafe is a good spot to grab a bite or a cold drink.

❼ Beaver Lake

Another 500m further south, the artificial pond **Lac aux Castors** (www.lemontroyal.qc.ca; 🚌11) is a haven of toy-boat captains in summer and ice-skaters in winter. Refreshments are available at the pavilion, and in warm weather the meadows around the pond are full of sunbathers.

Walking Tour

Touring Olympic Park & the Jardin Botanique

It's well worth making the trip out to the vast Olympic Park, which is home to an array of top attractions, including some magnificent botanical gardens, a planetarium, a kid-friendly ecosystems museum and an eye-popping stadium. The park surrounds the eponymous sporting arena, which was built for the 1976 Olympic Games.

Walk Facts

Start Biodôme; M Viau

End Jardin Botanique; M Pie-IX

Length 2km; four hours

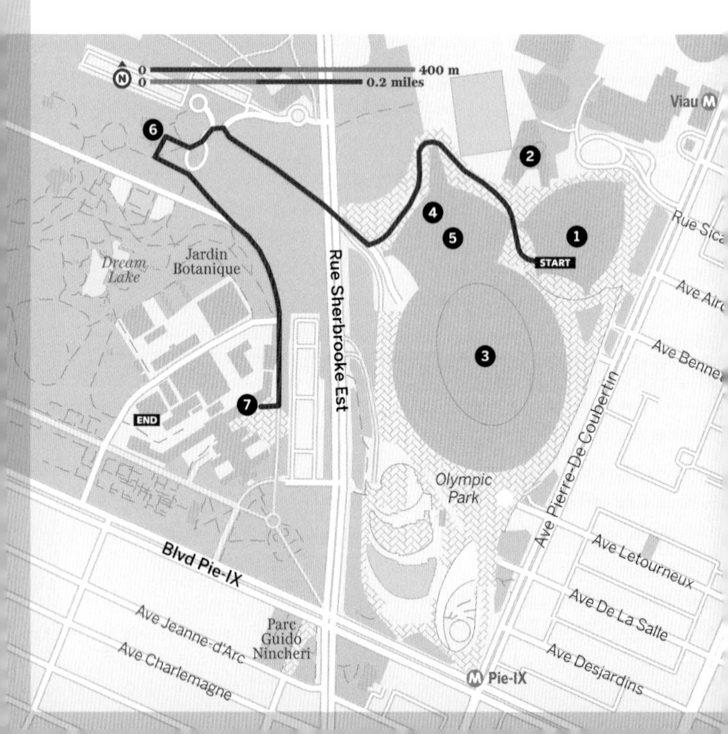

❶ Global Ecosystems

Start at the **Biodôme** (☎514-868-3000; www.espacepourlavie.ca/biodome; 4777 Ave du Pierre-De Coubertin; adult/child $20/10; ⏲9am-6pm late Jun-Sep, 9am-5pm Tue-Sun rest of year; 👪). Kids and adults alike can be absorbed by the recreations of five different natural environments – Antarctic islands, rainforests, rolling woodlands, aquatic life, or the raw Atlantic oceanfront.

❷ Into the Cosmos

Exit and ahead to your right you will see the metallic towers of the **Planétarium** (☎514-868-3000; 4801 Ave du Pierre-De Coubertin; adult/child $20/10; ⏲9am-5pm Sun, Tue & Wed, to 8pm Thu-Sat; 👪) where high-tech domed theaters and interactive exhibits bring outer space to you.

❸ Olympic Icon

Exit towards the tower, visible from anywhere in the area. You'll see the curve of the **Olympic Stadium** (Stade Olympique; ☎514-252-4141; http://parcolympique.qc.ca; 4141 Ave Pierre-De Coubertin; tower adult/child $24/12; ⏲1-6pm Mon, 9am-6pm Tue-Sun mid-Jun–early Sep, 9am-5pm rest of year) to your left. The stadium seats 56,000 and is an architectural marvel.

❹ Panoramic Views

A bilevel cable car goes up the Montréal Tower that lords over the stadium. It's the world's tallest inclined structure (165m at a 45-degree angle) and allows you to take in the whole park.

❺ Aquatic Allure

The **Centre Aquatique** (☎514-252-4141; http://parcolympique.qc.ca; 4141 Ave Pierre-de-Courbertin; adult/child $7/5.50; ⏲6am-9pm Mon-Fri, 8am-6pm Sat & Sun) has six pools, diving towers and a 20m-deep scuba pool. The competition pools at the Olympic Stadium are great for swimming laps.

❻ Insect Intrigue

Continue straight ahead, crossing the underpass to reach Rue Sherbrooke Est, then head right. The **Insectarium** (www.espacepourlavie.ca/insectarium; 4581 Rue Sherbrooke Est; adult/child $22/11; ⏲9am-6pm) houses an intriguing collection of creepy crawlies. An expanded section features a Vivarium with living species alongside plants.

❼ Fabulous Gardens

Walk South to the **Jardin Botanique** (☎514-872-1400; www.espacepourlavie.ca/jardin-botanique; 4101 Rue Sherbrooke Est; adult/child $21/10; ⏲9am-6pm mid-May–early Sep, 9am-5pm Tue-Sun early Sep–mid-May; 👪), the third-largest botanical garden in the world. The 75-hectare garden has thousands of different species in more than 20 thematic gardens, and its wealth of flowering plants is carefully managed to bloom in stages.

MARCHÉ JEAN-TA
www.marchespublics-mtl.c
VERGER
ÉRIC TANGUAY
ROUGEMONT
FERME
PETITS

Explore

Little Italy, Mile End & Outremont

Mile End and Outremont are two leafy neighborhoods where both upscale and old-world boutiques, restaurants and bars come together ever so fashionably, just up from the Plateau; nearby, Little Italy is a slice of the old world, with classic Italian trattorias and espresso bars, neighborhood churches and the sprawling Marché Jean-Talon (p94), the city's best market.

The Short List

- **Marché Jean-Talon (p94)** *Exploring the fresh produce, hawker stalls, and delightful seafood, sandwiches and desserts at Montréal's premiere market.*
- **Lawrence (p96)** *Spoiling yourself in Mile End with some of Montréal's best dining options.*
- **Caffè Italia (p95)** *Enjoying old-world pleasures by nursing an espresso in Little Italy.*

Getting There & Around

M Key stations are Laurier, Jean-Talon and Outremont.

Number 55 runs along Blvd St-Laurent; number 46 runs on part of Rue Bernard and Ave Laurier; bus 80 runs along Ave du Parc.

Little Italy, Mile End & Outremont Map on p92

Marché Jean-Talon (p94) HEMIS/ALAMY STOCK PHOTO ©

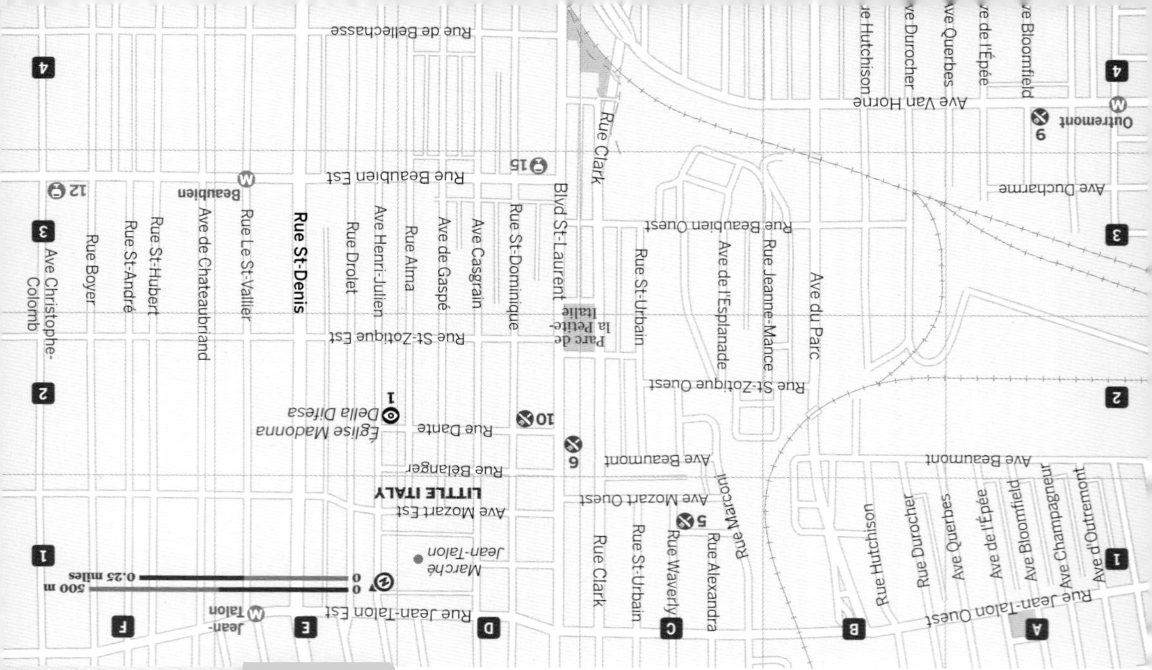

Rue Jean-Talon Ouest
Ave d'Outremont
Ave Champagneur
Ave Bloomfield
Ave de l'Épée
Ave Querbes
Rue Durocher
Rue Hutchison
Ave Beaumont
Rue Marconi
Rue Alexandra
Rue Waverly
Rue St-Urbain
Rue Clark
Ave Mozart Ouest
Ave Beaumont
Rue St-Zotique Ouest
Ave du Parc
Rue Jeanne-Mance
Ave de l'Esplanade
Rue Beaubien Ouest
Rue St-Urbain
Parc de la Petite-Italie
Rue Clark
Blvd St-Laurent
Rue St-Dominique
Ave Casgrain
Ave de Gaspé
Rue Alma
Ave Henri-Julien
Rue Drolet
Rue St-Denis
Rue Le St-Vallier
Ave de Chateaubriand
Rue St-Hubert
Rue St-André
Rue Boyer
Ave Christophe-Colomb
Rue Jean-Talon Est
Marché Jean-Talon
Ave Mozart Est
LITTLE ITALY
Rue Bélanger
Rue Dante
Église Madonna Della Difesa
Rue St-Zotique Est
Rue Beaubien Est
Rue de Bellechasse
Jean-Talon
Beaubien
Outremont
Ave Van Horne
Ave Ducharme
ve Bloomfield
ve de l'Épée
ve Querbes
ve Durocher
ue Hutchison
0
500 m
0
0.25 miles
A
B
C
D
E
F
1
2
3
4
1
5
6
9
10
12
15

Montréal Little Italy, Mile End & Outremont

For reviews see

Sights	p94
Eating	p94
Drinking	p97
Shopping	p99

OUTREMONT
MILE END
Parc Outremont 2
Parc St-Viateur 3
St-Viateur Bagel
Fairmount Bagel
Parc Lahaie
Parc St-Michel
Parc AT Lépine
Parc Sir Wilfred Laurier
Rosemont
Laurier
Ave Lajoie
Ave Outremont
Ave Champagneur
Ave Bloomfield
Ave Elmwood
Ave de l'Épée
Ave Querbes
Ave Durocher
Rue Hutchison
Ave du Parc
Rue Jeanne-Mance
Ave de l'Esplanade
Rue Waverly
Rue St-Urbain
Rue Clark
Blvd St-Laurent
Rue St-Dominique
Ave Casgrain
Ave de Gaspé
Ave Henri-Julien
Ave du Carmel
Rue Drolet
Rue St-Denis
Rue Rivard
Rue St-Grégoire
Rue Boucher
Rue Resther
Rue St-Hubert
Rue St-André
Rue de Mentana
Rue Boyer
Rue Maguire
Blvd St-Joseph Ouest
Blvd St-Joseph Est
Ave Laurier Ouest
Ave Laurier Est
Rue Labadie
Ave Fairmount Ouest
Ave Fairmount Est
Rue St-Viateur Ouest
Rue St-Viateur Est
Rue Bernard Ouest
Rue Bernard Est
Rue des Carrières
Viaduc Rosemont Van Horne
Blvd Rosemont

Marché Jean-Talon

The pride of Little Italy, this huge covered **market** (☎514-937-7754; www.marchespublics-mtl.com; 7075 Ave Casgrain; ⏰7am-6pm Mon-Wed & Sat, to 8pm Thu & Fri, to 5pm Sun; P 👪; Ⓜ Jean-Talon) is Montréal's most diverse. Many chefs buy ingredients here or in the specialty food shops nearby. Three long covered aisles are packed with merchants selling fruit, vegetables, flowers and baked goods, flanked by delis and cafe-restaurants. Even in winter, the market is open.

Sights

Église Madonna Della Difesa

CHURCH

1 MAP P92, E2

Our Lady of Protection Church was built in 1919 according to the drawings of Florence-born Guido Nincheri (1885–1973), who spent two decades working on the Roman Byzantine structure. The artist painted the church's remarkable frescoes, including one of Mussolini on horseback. The work honored the formal recognition by Rome of the pope's sovereignty over Vatican City in 1929 and was unveiled as Hitler came to power. (☎514-277-6522; www.facebook.com/MadonnadellaDifesaMTL; 6800 Ave Henri-Julien; ⏰Mass 8-11am Sun, 8am Mon, 7:30pm Tue-Fri; Ⓜ Jean-Talon)

Parc Outremont

PARK

2 MAP P92, A6

One of Montréal's best-kept secrets, this small leafy space is great for a bit of quiet time after exploring the neighborhood. Lovely Victorian homes ring the park, and benches provide a nice vantage point for viewing the small pond with fountain. This is a good spot to go to with an ice cream from **Le Bilboquet**, two blocks northwest. (☎514-276-0414; www.bilboquet.ca; 1311 Rue Bernard Ouest; cones $2.50-6; ⏰9am-midnight Jun-Aug, to 8pm mid-Mar–May & Sep-Dec, closed Jan–mid-Mar; Ⓜ Laurier, 🐾; Ⓜ Rosemont)

Parc St-Viateur

PARK

3 MAP P92, A5

Just off Rue Bernard a pedestrian lane leads to this small but handsomely landscaped neighborhood park. It has a bridge over a narrow circular waterway, which draws ice-skaters in winter (bring your own skates). (Ⓜ cnr Ave l'Épée & Rue Bernard)

Eating

Arts Cafe

INTERNATIONAL $

4 MAP P92, C7

The Arts Cafe has instant appeal with its plank floors, white clapboard walls and sculptural knickknacks (a frenzy of light bulbs above the windows, vintage farmhouse relics). But it's the all-day brunches/breakfasts that warrant the greatest amount of attention – excellent *fattoush*, falafel, *shakshuka* and cod cakes. Most dishes have a vegetarian option. (☎514-274-0919; http://artscafemontreal.com; 201 Ave Fairmount Ouest; mains $13-16; ⏱9am-6pm Mon-Fri, 10am-4pm Sat & Sun; ; M Laurier)

Dépanneur Le Pick Up DINER $

5 MAP P92, C1

A hip favorite, unpretentious Le Pick Up began as an authentic 1950s *dépanneur* (convenience store) and snack bar before the current owners took it over and added zines (homemade magazines) to the daily necessities on the shelves and '80s synth-pop to the stereo. Nosh on yummy veggie burgers, or grilled haloumi and pulled-pork sandwiches at the grill counter. (☎514-271-8011; http://depanneurlepickup.com; 7032 Rue Waverly; mains $5-9; ⏱7am-7pm Mon-Fri, 9am-7pm Sat, 10am-6pm Sun; ; M De Castelnau)

Caffè Italia CAFE $

6 MAP P92, D2

Calling this place old school is like calling the Sahara dry. 'Old school' isn't just a descriptor, but the essence of this little Italian espresso bar – graybeards and guys unironically wearing flat caps seemingly step out of a time warp for a quick coffee on the Formica counter. Grab a panettone and an espresso, and live that *dolce vita*. (☎514-495-0059; 6840 Blvd St-Laurent; sandwiches $8, coffees $2-3; ⏱6am-11pm; M De Castelnau)

Fresco of Mussolini by Guido Nincheri, Église Madonna Della Difesa

Sparrow

INTERNATIONAL $$

7 MAP P92, C7

In a vintage chic dining room, Mile Enders feast on mussels with white wine and fries, pan-roasted trout, butter chicken and other unfussy but tasty bistro classics. For the price, it's hard to find a better meal in this city. Sparrow serves up excellent cocktails, and the festive vibe continues until late into the night. (514-507-1642; http://lesparrowbar.com; 5322 Blvd St-Laurent; mains $10-16; 6pm-3am daily & 10am-3pm Sat & Sun; ; M Laurier)

Lawrence

EUROPEAN $$

8 MAP P92, D7

This gorgeously designed, high-style hip eatery helmed by British chef Marc Cohen of Sparrow serves up some of the best brunch in Montréal. With high windows looking out over the Main and an airy vibe, it's a perfect spot to sink your teeth into smoked trout with scrambled eggs or scones with jam and clotted cream. (514-503-1070; https://lawrencemtl.com/; 5201 Blvd St-Laurent; mains brunch $13-17, dinner $23-36; 11:30am-2:30pm Tue-Fri, 5:30-10pm Tue-Sat, 10am-2:30pm Sat & Sun; M Laurier)

Fairmount Bagel

HEMIS/ALAMY STOCK PHOTO ©

Damas Restaurant

SYRIAN $$$

9 MAP P92, A4

Unique Syrian-inspired cuisine just a few minutes from Mile End and Little Italy, Damas is consistently rated as one of the top restaurants in the city. A warm and welcoming ambience, along with an eclectic menu of Syrian classics (Damascus marinated chicken, tahini seabass), and inspiring new flavors (herbed dumplings, sumac fries), all come together for a complete fine-dining experience. (514-439-5435; www.restaurantdamas.com; 1201 Ave Van Horne; mains $34-62; 5-10pm Mon-Thu, to 11pm Fri, 4-11pm Sat, 4-10pm Sun; ; M Outremont)

Impasto

ITALIAN $$$

10 MAP P92, D2

There's much buzz surrounding this polished Italian eatery, largely owing to the heavy-hitting foodies behind it: best-selling cookbook author Stefano Faita and celebrated chef Michele Forgione. Both have deep connections to Italian cooking, obvious in brilliant dishes such as

The Great Bagel Debate

The Montréal bagel has a long and venerable history. It all started in 1915 when Isadore and Fanny Shlafman, Jews from Ukraine, opened a tiny bakery on Rue Roy in the Plateau. They made the yeast bread rings according to a recipe they'd brought from the bakery where Shlafman's father worked. In 1919 they started the Montréal Bagel Bakery in a wooden shack just off Blvd St-Laurent, a few doors down from the Plateau's iconic **Schwartz's** (p81) deli.

After WWII many Holocaust survivors emigrated to Montréal and the bagel market boomed. Isadore Shlafman decided to build a bakery in the living room of his house at 74 Ave Fairmount, where he opened **Fairmount Bagel** (Map p93, C7; 514-272-0667; http://fairmountbagel.com; 74 Ave Fairmount Ouest; bagels $1; 24hr; M Laurier) in 1950. Meanwhile Myer Lewkowicz, a Polish Jew who had survived Auschwitz, went on to establish **St-Viateur Bagel** (Map p92, B6; 514-276-8044; www.stviateurbagel.com; 263 Rue St-Viateur Ouest; bagels 90¢; 24hr; M Place-des-Arts, then 80) in 1957. A legendary rivalry was born and scores of other bagel bakeries sprang up in their wake.

Most locals believe that Montréal's bagels are superior to their New York cousins. The Montréal bagel is lighter, sweeter and crustier, and chewy but not dense. The dough hardly rises and the tender rings are formed by hand and boiled in a honey-and-water solution before baking in a wood-burning oven.

braised beef cheeks with Savoy-style potatoes, arctic char with cauliflower puree and lentils, and housemade pastas like *busiate* with lobster. (514-508-6508; www.impastomtl.ca; 48 Rue Dante; mains $19-36; 11:30am-2pm Thu & Fri, 5-11pm Tue-Sat; M De Castelnau)

Drinking

La Remise — PUB

11 MAP P92, F7

If you want to catch a cool crowd belting out a francophone classic, head straight to this dive bar (it is heartland Mile End after all). There are English hits on the playlist, too. Cheap drinks and a pool table help make it friendly to visitors; so does the very very dark lighting. (514-272-0206; 540 Rue Boucher; 11am-3am; M Laurier)

Isle de Garde — BAR

12 MAP P92, F3

Beer lovers shouldn't miss this buzzing amber-lit brasserie, which has a dazzling (and ever-changing) selection of unique microbrews on tap. Friendly bar staff dole out Belgian-style farmhouse ales,

American-style IPAs and creamy stouts, with one-of-a-kind brews (such as Brasseurs Illimités smoked porter that tastes like drinking a campfire) among the options. (www.isledegarde.com; 1039 Rue Beaubien Est; 1pm-1:30am Sun-Wed, 11:30am-3am Thu & Fri, 1pm-3am Sat; ; M Beaubien)

Bar Waverly

BAR

13 MAP P92, C6

With its engaging decor and a great location, Bar Waverly has established itself in the Mile End bar scene. A full selection of cocktails is complemented by a tasty and well-priced food menu. Sit outside on the large patio or enjoy a drink in the warm-yet-happening indoor ambience. Good for a relaxed happy hour or some late-night fun. (http://barwaverly.com; 5550 Blvd St-Laurent; 4pm-3am; M Laurier)

Bar Datcha

CLUB

14 MAP P92, C8

Datcha is a small night spot with a tiny dance floor that draws a laid-back, groove-loving crowd enveloped in the fog machine. Eclectic DJs from around the globe spin here, and on Thursdays you can groove to jazz while having your tarot read. Party like it's 1987, while sipping Moscow Mules (vodka, ginger syrup, lime juice) from the adjoining bar **Kabinet** (514-274-3555; www.barkabinet.com; 98 Ave Laurier Ouest; 5pm-1am Mon, 4pm-2am Tue & Wed, 4pm-3am Thu & Fri, 3pm-3am Sat, 3pm-1am Sun). (www.bardatcha.ca; 98 Ave Laurier Ouest; 10pm-3am Thu-Sun; M Laurier)

Notre Dame des Quilles

BAR

15 MAP P92, D3

Does drinking improve your bowling game? That seems to be the eternal question at this hip outpost near Little Italy, where two free lanes have been set up with pint-sized pins. There's a good mix of anglophones and francophones here, and there are fun kitsch-filled nights of karaoke, bingo and spinning DJs. (514-507-1313; www.facebook.com/notredamedesquilles; 32 Rue Beaubien Est; 5pm-3am Mon-Fri, from 4pm Sat & Sun; M Beaubien)

Café Olimpico

CAFE

16 MAP P92, C6

Its espresso is excellent, yet this rocking, no-frills Italian cafe is all about atmosphere, as young good-looking baristas whip up smooth caffeinated drinks for the jumble of hipsters, tourists and elderly gentlemen who pass through. It's big on sports (especially the Italian football league), so there are TVs inside. (514-495-0746; 124 Rue St-Viateur; coffees $2-4; 7am-midnight; ; M Laurier)

Café Olimpico

Shopping

Drawn & Quarterly BOOKS

17 MAP P92, C5

The flagship store of this cult independent comic-book and graphic-novel publisher has become something of a local literary haven. Cool book launches take place here, and the quaint little shop sells all sorts of reading matter, including children's books, vintage Tintin comics, recent fiction and art books. (514-279-2224; http://mtl.drawnandquarterly.com; 211 Rue Bernard Ouest; 10am-8pm; M Outremont)

Au Papier Japonais ARTS & CRAFTS

18 MAP P92, C7

You might never guess how many guises Japanese paper can come in until you visit this gorgeous little shop, which stocks more than 800 varieties. Origami kits and art books make great gifts, as do the elegant teapots, pottery and Buddha boards (where you can 'paint' ephemeral works with water). (514-276-6863; www.aupapierjaponais.com; 24 Ave Fairmount Ouest; 10am-6pm Mon-Sat, noon-4pm Sun; M Laurier)

Explore

Lachine Canal & Little Burgundy

This area has at its heart the Marché Atwater and the adjacent Canal de Lachine, one of the best cycling paths in the whole of the city and a top picnic spot. The surrounding working-class districts Little Burgundy (Petite-Bourgogne), St-Henri and Monkland Village have excellent eating and good coffee, with a bohemian vibe that is now tipping into gentrified.

The Short List

- ***Habitat 67 (p105)*** *Puzzling over the retro-futuristic hive architecture of portside apartments made for Expo 67.*
- ***Canal de Lachine (p102)*** *Walking or cycling off those poutine calories along 14km of bike paths and green spaces.*
- ***Marché Atwater (p105)*** *Savoring fresh produce and tasty international food stalls inside one of Montréal's best markets.*
- ***Joe Beef (p108)*** *Feasting on creative, market-fresh fare in this Little Burgundy gem.*

Getting There & Around

M Handy stations include Lionel-Groulx for the Little Burgundy and the Atwater Market and Villa-Maria for Notre-Dame-de-Grâce.

You can rent a Bixi bike to reach NDG, Petite-Bourgogne, St-Henri and Pointe-St-Charles, and to roll along the Canal de Lachine. Bikes are best avoided in hilly Côte-des-Neiges.

Lachine Canal & Little Burgundy Map on p104

Canal de Lachine

Cycling Tour

Cycling the Canal de Lachine

A perfect marriage of urban infrastructure and green civic planning: a 14km-long cycling and pedestrian pathway, with picnic areas and outdoor spaces. Since the canal was reopened for navigation in 2002, flotillas of pleasure boats glide along its calm waters. The Lachine Canal was built in 1825 as a means of bypassing the treacherous Lachine Rapids on the St Lawrence River.

Cycle Facts

Start Canal Locks; M Square-Victoria–OACI

End Canal Locks; M Square-Victoria–OACI

Length 7km; two hours

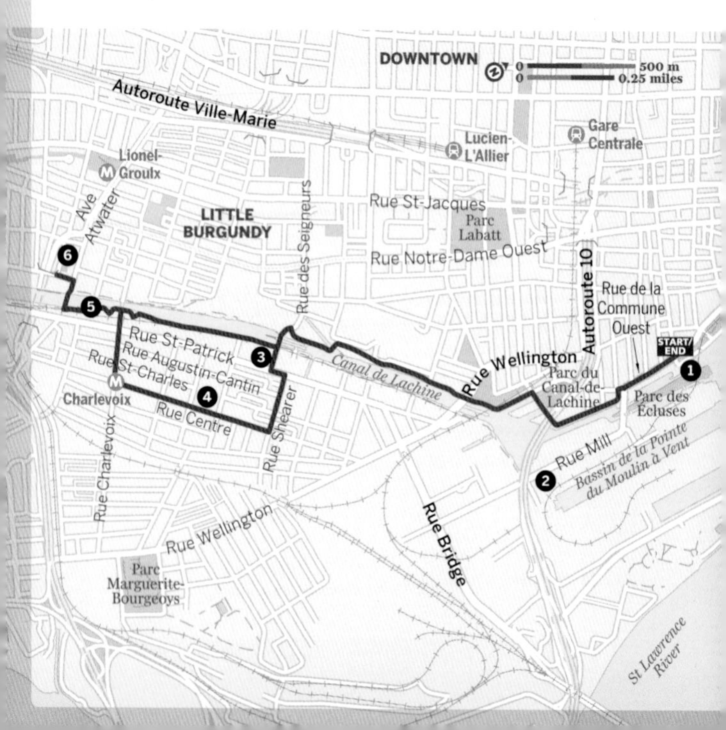

❶ Old Port

Start off your cycle at the peaceful Canal Locks which are located at the southwestern end of the Old Port. This area has an industrial feel to it thanks to the abandoned grain silo to the southeast of the locks.

❷ Industrial Icon

Pedaling southwest along Rue de la Commune Ouest, you'll pass under Autoroute 10. Continue cycling along the downtown side of the canal, which is lined with strips of greenery. The enormous neon sign Farine Five Roses crowns a former flour mill across the canal.

❸ Urban Renewal

The path switches sides at the bridge at Rue des Seigneurs, where you will come to a former silk mill that ran its operations on hydraulic power from the canal. The red-brick factory has since been reborn as lofts.

❹ Ecclesiastical Landmarks

Continue cycling south on Rue Shearer and turn right on Rue Centre. You'll come to the Romanesque Église St-Charles on your right. Push your bike over to the French-style Église St-Gabriel, taking in all of the charms of this seldom-visited neighborhood.

❺ On the Water

Once you're done exploring, carry on to Rue Charlevoix, turn right and you'll soon be on the bike path once again. Turn left, and you'll come to **H2O Adventures** (514-842-1306; www.h2oadventures.com; 2727b Rue St-Patrick; pedal boat/tandem kayak/electric boat/voyageur canoe per hour $25/35/50/50; 9am-9pm Jun-Aug, noon-7:30pm Mon-Fri, 10am-7:30pm Sat & Sun Sep-May; M Charlevoix), a kayak-rental outfit. If you're interested in getting out on the water, this is the place to do it. Don't fancy kayaking? Electric boats are also available to rent here.

❻ Grand Market

Continue on the bike path and then turn right at the pedestrian bridge to head to Marché Atwater (p105), one of the best markets in the whole of the city. After you've browsed to your heart's content, assemble a picnic of delicious breads, cheeses and other tasty snacks here to enjoy by the water where there are green spaces and convinient outdoor picnic tables. Once you've eaten your fill, take an easy pedal back to your starting point.

For reviews see
Sights p105
Eating p106
Drinking p108
Shopping p109
0 400 m
0 0.2 miles
Canal de Lachine
Autoroute Ville-Marie
LITTLE BURGUNDY
ST-HENRI
Lionel-Groulx
Place-St-Henri
Parc Vinet
Parc Sir-George-Étienne-Cartier
Marché Atwater
Canal Lounge
Antique Alley
Rue St-Patrick
Rue Dominion
Rue Ste-Cunégonde
Rue Duvernay
Rue Charlevoix
Rue de Lévis
Rue Rufus Rockhead
Ave Atwater
Rue Ste-Émilie
Rue Rose de Lima
Rue Bourget
Rue Turgeon
Rue St-Augustin
Rue St-Ambroise
Rue Workman
Rue Vinet
Rue Delisle
Ave Lionel Groulx
Rue Notre-Dame Ouest
Rue St-Jacques
Rue Quesnel
Rue Coursol
Ave Marin
Ave Walker
Ave Greene
Ave Brewster
Rue Bel Air
Rue Irène
Ave Laporte
Rue Agnès
Rue du Couvent
Rue St-Ferdinand
Rue St-Philippe
Rue Ste-Marguerite
Rue Beaudoin
Rue St-Émilie
Sq Sir-Georges-Étienne-Cartier
Rue Delinelle
Rue de Courcelle
Rue St-Antoine Ouest

Sights

Marché Atwater
MARKET

1 MAP P104, D3

Just off the Canal de Lachine, this fantastic market has a mouthwatering assortment of fresh produce from local farms (some promoting sustainability), excellent wines, crusty breads, fine cheeses and other delectable fare. The market's specialty shops operate year-round, while outdoor eatery stalls open from March to October. It's all housed in a 1933 brick hall, topped with a clock tower, and little bouts of live music pop off with pleasing regularity. The grassy banks overlooking the canal are great for a picnic. (514-937-7754; www.marchespublics-mtl.com; 138 Ave Atwater; 7am-6pm Mon-Wed, to 7pm Thu, to 8pm Fri, to 5pm Sat & Sun; M Atwater)

Habitat 67
NOTABLE BUILDING

2 MAP P104, F4

The artificial peninsula Cité-du-Havre was created to protect the port from vicious currents and ice. Here, in 1967, architect Moshe Safdie designed a set of futuristic cube-like condominiums for Expo 67 when he was just 23 years old – from a distance, they resemble a microscopic zoom-in on table salt. This narrow spit of land connects Île Ste-Hélène with Old Montréal via the Pont de la Concorde. (514-866-5971; www.habitat67.com; 2600 Ave Pierre Dupuy; tours adult/child under 12yr $25/free; tours Tue-Sat May-Oct)

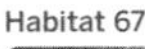
Habitat 67

Centre Canadien d'Architecture

A must for architecture fans, this **center** (www.cca.qc.ca; 1920 Rue Baile; adult/child $10/free, 5:30-9pm Thu & 1st Sun of month free; 11am-6pm Wed-Sun, to 9pm Thu; M Georges-Vanier) is equal parts museum and research institute. The building incorporates Shaughnessy House, a 19th-century gray limestone treasure. Highlights in this section include the conservatory and an ornate sitting room with intricate woodwork and a massive stone fireplace. The exhibition galleries focus on remarkable architectural works of both local and international scope.

Eating

Satay Brothers

MALAYSIAN $

3 MAP P104, D2

Amid red walls, hanging lamps and mismatched thrift-store furnishings, this lively and Malaysia-chic bar-bistro serves some of the best 'street food' in Montréal. Crowds flock here to gorge on delicious chicken-satay sandwiches, tangy green papaya salad, braised pork (or tofu) buns, and *laksa lemak*, a rich and spicy coconut soup. (514-933-3507; www.sataybrothers.com; 3721 Rue Notre-Dame Ouest; mains $9-15; 11am-11pm Wed-Sun; M Lionel-Groulx)

Kazu

JAPANESE $

4 MAP P104, F1

Kazuo Akutsu's frenetic hole-in-the-wall in the Concordia Chinatown draws long lines of people waiting for *gyoza* (dumplings), ramen-noodle soup and awesome creations such as the 48-hour pork. Its popularity is well earned, but be warned: it gets cramped inside. (514-937-2333; www.kazumontreal.com; 1862 Rue Ste-Catherine Ouest; mains $10-17; noon-3pm Sun, Mon, Thu & Fri, also 5:30-9:30pm Thu-Mon; M Guy-Concordia)

Le Vin Papillon

INTERNATIONAL $$

5 MAP P104, E3

The folks behind Joe Beef (p108) continue the hit parade with this delightful wine bar and small-plate eatery next door to Liverpool House – another Joe Beef success. Creative, mouthwatering veggie dishes take top billing with favorites such as tomato-and-chickpea salad, sautéed chanterelles and smoked-eggplant caviar, along with roasted cauliflower with chicken skin, guinea-fowl confit, and charcuterie and cheese platters. (www.vinpapillon.com; 2519 Rue Notre-Dame Ouest; small plates $7-17; 3pm-midnight Tue-Sat; ; M Lionel-Groulx)

Foiegwa

QUÉBÉCOIS $$

6 MAP P104, E2

Foiegwa is a trendy Québécois-French fusion restaurant dressed in the aesthetic of a classic diner. Taking over the location of a long-time neighborhood greasy spoon, it serves decadent dishes with a casual touch. Poutine, gourmet burgers and more feature foie gras (typically duck or goose liver produced by force-feeding). Cozy seating, hand-crafted cocktails and a lively ambience. (438-387-4252; http://foiegwa.com; 3001 Rue Notre-Dame Ouest; mains $15-25; 5pm-2am; M Lionel Groulx)

Su

TURKISH $$

7 MAP P104, D4

Chef Fisun Ercan takes her home-style but inventive Turkish cuisine beyond your expectations of kabobs and coffee. She prepares feather-light fried calamari, beef *manti* (dumplings) with garlic yogurt and spiced tomatoes, rich seafood rice (with shrimp, mussels and fish) and delicious *lokum* (Turkish delight). It's worth the trip to Verdun; be sure to reserve. (514-362-1818; www.restaurantsu.com; 5145 Rue Wellington; mains $18-26; 5-10:30pm Tue-Wed, to 11pm Thu-Sun, also 10am-3pm Sat & Sun; M Verdun)

Liverpool House

QUÉBÉCOIS $$$

8 MAP P104, F3

Liverpool House sets the standard so many Québec restaurants are racing for: a laid-back ambience that feels like a friend's dinner party, where the food is sent from angels on high. Expect oysters, smoked trout, braised rabbit, lobster spaghetti and other iterations of regional excellence. There is usually a vegetarian main, but sometimes just one choice. (514-313-6049; www.joebeef.ca; 2501 Rue Notre-Dame Ouest; mains $24-50; 5-11pm Tue-Sat;)

Tuck Shop

QUÉBÉCOIS $$$

9 MAP P104, A2

Set in the heart of working-class St-Henri, Tuck Shop could have been plucked from London or New York if it weren't for its distinctly local menu, a delightful blend of market and terroir (locally sourced) offerings such as Kamouraska lamb shank, fish of the day with Jerusalem-artichoke puree and a Québec cheese plate, all prepared by able chef Theo Lerikos. (514-439-7432; www.tuckshop.ca; 4662 Rue Notre-Dame Ouest; mains $30-36; 5-11pm Tue-Sat; ; M Place-St-Henri)

Bike Hire

For a canal-side spin departing from Old Montréal, one of the best places to hire bikes is at **Ça Roule Montréal** (514-866-0633; www.caroulemontreal.com; 27 Rue de la Commune Est; bikes per hour/day from $9/40, in-line skates 1st/additional hour $9/4; 9am-7pm, reduced hours winter; M Place-d'Armes). It also has kids' bikes, tandems and trailers, as well as in-line skates.

Joe Beef

QUÉBÉCOIS $$$

10 MAP P104, F3

In the heart of the Little Burgundy neighborhood, Joe Beef remains a darling of food critics for its unfussy, market-fresh fare. The rustic, country-kitsch setting is a great spot to linger over fresh oysters, braised rabbit, roasted scallops with smoked onions and a changing selection of hearty Québécois dishes – all served with good humor and low pretension. (514-935-6504; www.joebeef.ca; 2491 Rue Notre-Dame Ouest; mains $30-55; 6pm-late Tue-Sat; M Lionel-Groulx)

Canal Lounge

This permanently docked **boat-bar** (Map p104, D4; 514-451-2665; www.canallounge.com; 22 Ave Atwater; 3-11pm Tue-Sat, to 10pm Sun late May-early Oct; M Lionel Groulx) nestles along the canal in front of a lovely pedestrian bridge. The over-45-year-old vessel has been converted into an upscale cocktail lounge. Sit on the rooftop for some fresh air or inside for maritime ambience. The friendly owners moonlight as bartenders and whip up finely crafted cocktails.

Drinking

La Drinkerie Ste-Cunégonde

BAR

11 MAP P104, E3

Along the popular Rue Notre-Dame you'll find this locally owned bar that's perfect for a relaxing evening drink or a late-night party. Well-crafted cocktails, original menu options, and a summertime patio have made La Drinkerie a popular spot with Little Burgundy and St-Henri residents. Walking distance from the Lachine Canal, the Marché Atwater and many restaurant options. (www.facebook.com/Drinkerie; 2661 Rue Notre-Dame Ouest; 3pm-3am; M Lionel Groulx)

Café Lili & Oli

COFFEE

12 MAP P104, E3

This family-owned cafe is a Little Burgundy mainstay, delivering delicious coffee and a welcoming ambience. Freshly baked muffins and one of the best iced coffees in town are just some of the highlights. Bring your dog or your laptop and hang out with some locals, chances are you'll be charmed. (www.facebook.com/liliandoli; 2713 Rue Notre-Dame Ouest; 7am-10pm Mon-Thu, to 8pm Fri, 8am-8pm Sat & Sun; ; M Lionel Groulx)

Marché Atwater (p105)

Burgundy Lion

PUB

13 MAP P104, F3

This trendy take on the traditional English pub features British pub fare, beers and whiskeys galore, and an attitude-free vibe where everyone (and their parents) feels welcome to sit and drink, eat and be merry. Things tend to get the good kind of crazy on late-night weekends at the Burgundy Lion. Tip your cap to Queen Elizabeth, whose portrait adorns the bathroom door. (514-934-0888; www.burgundylion.com; 2496 Rue Notre-Dame Ouest; 11:30am-3am Mon-Fri, 9am-3am Sat & Sun; M Lionel-Groulx)

Shopping

Marché Underground

VINTAGE

14 MAP P104, C2

Vintage doesn't have to mean pricey, especially outside of Mile End and the Plateau. Visit this collective of nearly 10 sellers of clothes, furniture, toys, homewares and other collectibles from yesteryear. You'll pay close to what you would pay at thrift stores, but here it's all pleasingly curated so you can shop with ease. (514-820-2117; https://marche-underground.business.site; 3731 Rue Notre-Dame Ouest; noon-6pm Mon-Wed, to 9pm Thu, to 5pm Fri, 11am-5pm Sat & Sun; M Lionel-Groulx)

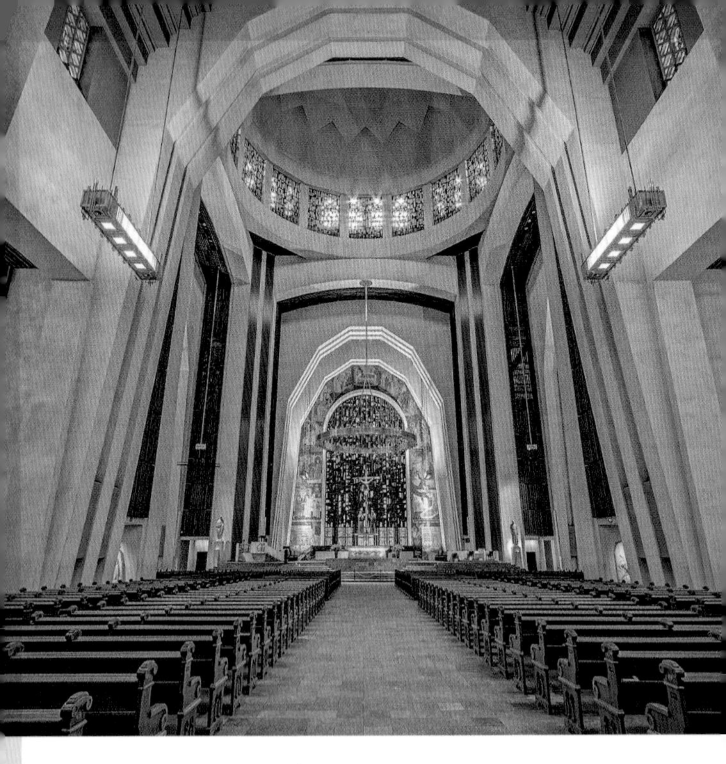

Top Experience

Take in the Views From Oratoire St-Joseph

This stunning church (pictured) built on the flanks of Mont-Royal commands grand views of the Côte-des-Neiges area and northwest Montréal. The majestic basilica is a tribute to mid-20th-century design as well as an intimate shrine to Brother André, a local saint said to have healed countless people.

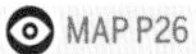
MAP P26

St-Joseph's Oratory

www.saint-joseph.org

3800 Chemin Queen-Mary

$3, 2-for-1 entry with Opus card P $5

24hr

M Laurier, then 51

Fine Views

The largest shrine ever built in honor of Jesus' earthly father, this Renaissance-style building was completed in 1960 and commands fine views of the northern slope of Mont-Royal. The oratory dome is visible from anywhere in this part of town.

Healing Powers

The oratory is also a tribute to the work of Brother André (1845–1937), the determined monk who first built a little chapel here in 1904. Brother André was said to have healing powers – as word spread, a larger shrine was needed, so the church began gathering funds to build one. Rows of discarded crutches and walking sticks in the basement Votive Chapel testify to this belief and the shrine is warmed by hundreds of candles. When Brother André died at age 91, a million devotees filed past his coffin over the course of six days. His black granite tomb in the Votive Chapel was donated by Québec premier Maurice Duplessis. Brother André was beatified in 1982 and finally canonized in 2010. His heart is on display too, in an upstairs museum dedicated to him.

Climb the Steps

Religious pilgrims might climb the 300 wooden steps to the oratory on their knees, praying at every step; other visitors take the stone stairs or one of the free shuttle buses from the base parking lot.

Explore the Garden

To the east of the basilica is a little-visited garden with water features, a small greenhouse and sculptures for meditation in a natural surrounding.

★ Top Tips

- A free organ concert takes place in the main church here most Sunday afternoons.
- Bring your Opus card for 2-for-1 entry.
- The oratory is open 24 hours; visit at night for serene reflection.
- For the best views, take the stone stairs rather than the shuttle bus.
- Take a summer guided tour to really bring the story of the oratory to life.

Take a Break

There is a coffee shop serving breakfast, light meals and pastries on level 5 of Oratoire St-Joseph; vending machines have snacks.

Outside the oratory grounds, there's nowhere to eat nearby.

Québec City Neighborhoods

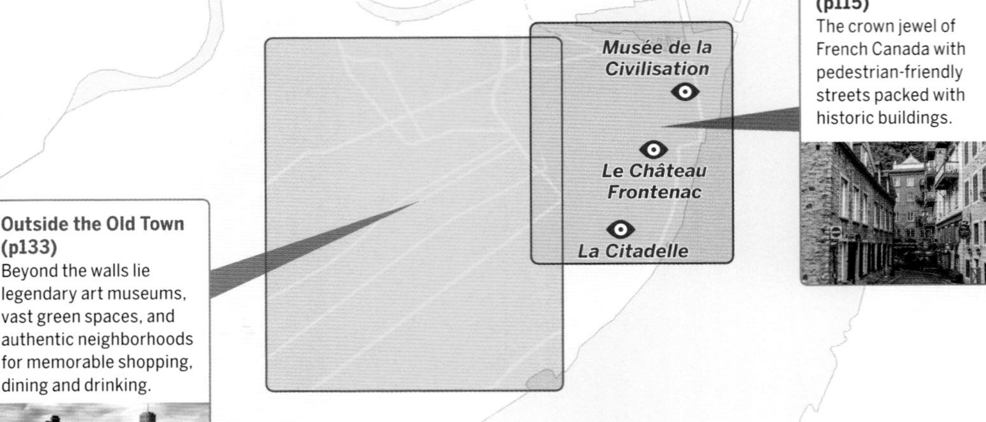

Old Town & Port (p115)
The crown jewel of French Canada with pedestrian-friendly streets packed with historic buildings.

Outside the Old Town (p133)
Beyond the walls lie legendary art museums, vast green spaces, and authentic neighborhoods for memorable shopping, dining and drinking.

Explore Québec City

Situated on a cliff high above the St Lawrence River, Québec City offers great food, picturesque streets and old-world charm. It also boasts a wide range of museums and galleries, and the opportunity to delve deeper into the history and culture of Canada's French-speaking province.

Québec City's Walking Tours

La
Chasse-Galerie
Boutique

Explore Old Town & Port

Québec City's picturesque Old Town is a Unesco World Heritage site, a living museum of narrow cobblestone streets, 17th- and 18th-century houses and soaring church spires, with the splendid Château Frontenac hotel and city icon towering above it all. There's more than a glimmer of Old Europe in its classic bistros, sidewalk cafes and manicured squares.

The Short List

- ***Le Quartier Petit-Champlain (p126)*** *Taking in the 17th-century architecture, inviting cafes and outdoor art in one of Québec City's prettiest districts.*
- ***Musée de la Civilisation (p120)*** *Learning about indigenous culture in fascinating exhibitions that span 2000 years.*
- ***Terrasse Dufferin (p126)*** *Enjoying the spectacular sweeping views over the St Lawrence River from this long boardwalk.*
- ***La Citadelle (p116)*** *Taking a lantern-lit tour through one of Canada's most imposing fortresses.*
- ***Le Château Frontenac (p118)*** *Admiring Québec City's most striking building, inside and out.*

Getting There & Around

RTC bus 1 links the Old Lower Town with the Gare du Palais train and bus stations.

Connects the Old Upper and Lower Towns (or you can take the stairs).

Old Town & Port Map on p124

Old Town view to Le Château Frontenac HONESTTRAVELLER/GETTY IMAGES ©

Top Experience

Discover Québec's Military History at La Citadelle

Towering above the St Lawrence River, this massive, star-shaped fort (pictured) is a living museum that offers something for all ages. The exhibits on military life from colonial times to today will appeal to anyone interested in Québécois history, while children will be enthralled by special costumed events.

MAP P124, C7

418-694-2815

www.lacitadelle.qc.ca

Côte de la Citadelle

adult/child $16/6

9am-5pm May-Oct, 10am-4pm Nov-Apr

Historical Roots

French forces started building a defensive structure here in the late 1750s, but what we see today was constructed over 30 years from 1820 by the British, who feared two things: one, an American invasion of the colony and two, a possible revolt by the French-speaking population (that's why the cannons point not only at the river, but at Québec City itself).

By the time the Citadelle was completed, things were begining to calm down. In 1871, the Treaty of Washington between the United States and the newly minted Dominion of Canada ended the threat of an American invasion.

The Vandoos

The Citadelle today houses about 200 members of the Royal 22e Régiment, The Vandoos, which is a nickname taken from the French for 22 (vingt-deux), is the only entirely French-speaking battalion in the Canadian Forces and you will find a museum dedicated to them here. The second official residence of the governor general, who represents the Queen of England in Canada, has also been located here since 1872.

Tours

Hour-long guided tours of the Citadelle are excellent and will give you the lowdown on all of the spectacular architecture; make sure that you don't miss the King's Bastion with its nine-ton cannon and the *réduit* (fortification) used later as a military prison. From late June through October, lantern-lit evening tours are also offered so you can explore for longer.

★ Top Tips

- In summer, see the changing of the guard (daily at 10am) and the beating of the retreat (6pm Saturday).
- In the fort, visit the **Governor General's residence** on free tours; advance booking is required outside of June to early September. www.gg.ca/en/visit-us/rideau-hall/what-see-and-do/residence
- Explore Québec City's defenses by walking the 4.6km circuit around the walls.

Take a Break

Aux Anciens Canadiens (418-692-1627; www.auxancienscanadiens.qc.ca; 34 Rue St-Louis; mains $33-89; noon-9pm) serves traditional Québécois fare.

Near Porte St-Louis, **Apsara** (418-694-0232; http://restaurantapsara.com; 71 Rue d'Auteuil; mains $17-21; 11:30am-2pm Mon-Fri, 5:30-11pm daily, closed Mon winter) serves tasty Southeast Asian cuisine.

Top Experience

Grab a Fancy Seat at Le Château Frontenac's Bar or Bistro

This audaciously elegant structure is Québec City's most iconic edifice. Its fabulous turrets, winding hallways and imposing wings graciously complement its dramatic location atop Cap Diamant, a cliff that swoops into the St Lawrence River.

MAP P124, D5

418-692-3861

www.fairmont.com/frontenac-quebec

1 Rue des Carrières

The Design

Designed by New Yorker Bruce Price (father of manners maven Emily Post), the château was named after the mercurial Count of Frontenac, Louis de Buade, who governed New France in the late 1600s. Completed in 1893, it was one of the Canadian Pacific Railway's series of luxury hotels built across Canada.

History

In August 1943 and again in September 1944, the Québec Conferences involving British Prime Minister Winston Churchill, US President Franklin Roosevelt and Canadian Prime Minister William Lyon Mackenzie King were all held here to plot the final stages of WWII.

Since then, it's lured a never-ending line-up of luminaries, including Alfred Hitchcock, who shot the opening scene of his 1953 mystery *I Confess* here. Other illustrious guests have included people such as King George VI, Chiang Kai-shek, Princess Grace of Monaco and Paul McCartney.

Exploring the Interior

The Château Frontenac is probably one of the rare hotels where most people in the lobby (pictured) aren't even guests but rather tourists visiting to get close to the history and architecture (they say that this is the world's most photographed hotel).

Guided tours of the building were discontinued in 2011, but nonguests can still wander through the reception area (there's usually a special exhibition of some sort going on) and stop for a drink or a bite at the hotel's restaurant, bistro or bar.

★ Top Tips

- Book a tour with **Québec Cicerone Tours** (418-977-8977, 855-977-8977; www.cicerone.ca/en; 12 Rue Ste-Anne; adult/youth/child $20/10/free; Château Frontenac tour 10am, 1pm & 3pm late Jun–mid-Oct).
- Be sure to take a stroll along the nearby **Terrasse Dufferin** (p126) around sunset.
- Stop by the leafy **Jardin des Gouverneurs** (Rue Mont Carmel), located near the Château Frontenac. Even in peak season, it's a peaceful refuge from the holidaying masses.

Take a Break

Cheese lovers shouldn't miss the delightful *fromage* at **1608** (p128).

Grand views and brilliant cuisine await diners at high-end **Restaurant Champlain** (418-692-3861; www.restaurantchamplain.com; 1 Rue des Carrières, Fairmont Le Château Frontenac; mains $29-47; 6-9pm Tue-Sat, 10am-1pm Sun).

Top Experience

Learn About the People of Québec at the Musée de la Civilisation

This world-class museum wows even before you've clapped your eyes on the exhibits. It is a fascinating mix of modern design that incorporates preexisting industrial buildings along the old port with contemporary architecture. What's inside is quite unique in that this is really the only museum in town that regularly looks at contemporary issues and culture.

MAP P124, E3
Museum of Civilization
418-643-2158
www.mcq.org/en
85 Rue Dalhousie
adult/teen/child $17/6/free
10am-5pm mid-Jun–early Sep, closed Mon early Sep–mid-Jun

People of Québec: Then & Now

The grandiose-sounding 'Museum of Civilization' contains just two permanent exhibits. The first – and arguably more ambitious – is 'People of Québec: Then and Now,' which traces the history of the city and province imaginatively via multimedia from earliest times (12,500 BC) until today. It's a must-see for understanding Québec today; the postwar drive for an independent Québec is handled both sensitively and accurately.

This Is Our Story

The second permanent exhibit, called 'This Is Our Story' (pictured), focuses on the province's Aboriginals today – 93,000 people from a dozen different indigenous groups. The beautiful objects on display are unique, sensitively curated and highly educational, with some clever interactive elements. Listen to some of the interviews conducted with various members; they are interesting and enlightening.

Special Exhibits

The museum's focus on contemporary issues and culture sees some stunning special exhibits examining topics as diverse as London and its culture relating to Brexit, the transformation of Québec City from a city of trappers to one of entrepreneurs, and the social history of Québec and the Québécois in 400 very ordinary objects.

★ Top Tips

- Take a close look at the ancient stone steps and walls in the lobby: this was the early French port. The boat on display is one of a dozen found here when the museum was being built in the 1980s.
- The elegant Rue St-Pierre nearby is dotted with intriguing shops and makes a fine setting for a stroll.
- Be sure to stop by Place des Canotiers (a few steps south of the museum). This open-air space has photogenic views of both the St-Lawrence and the hilltop Château Frontenac.

Take a Break

The museum's Café 47 has hearty plates of poutine, pasta and fish and chips, as well as sandwiches and wraps.

Le Café du Monde (p128) has excellent bistro fare and a waterside location.

Walking Tour

Historic Stroll Through the Old Town

This historical walking tour encompasses a mix of well-known and lesser-known Vieux-Québec attractions. As you wind along the narrow lanes, you'll pass architectural treasures from the 17th to the 19th centuries, enjoy waterfront panoramas and get an eyeful of the old city's greatest mural. Start off early, before tour buses fill the streets.

Walk Facts

Start Porte St-Louis; 11

End Fresque des Québécois; 11

Length 3km; one to two hours

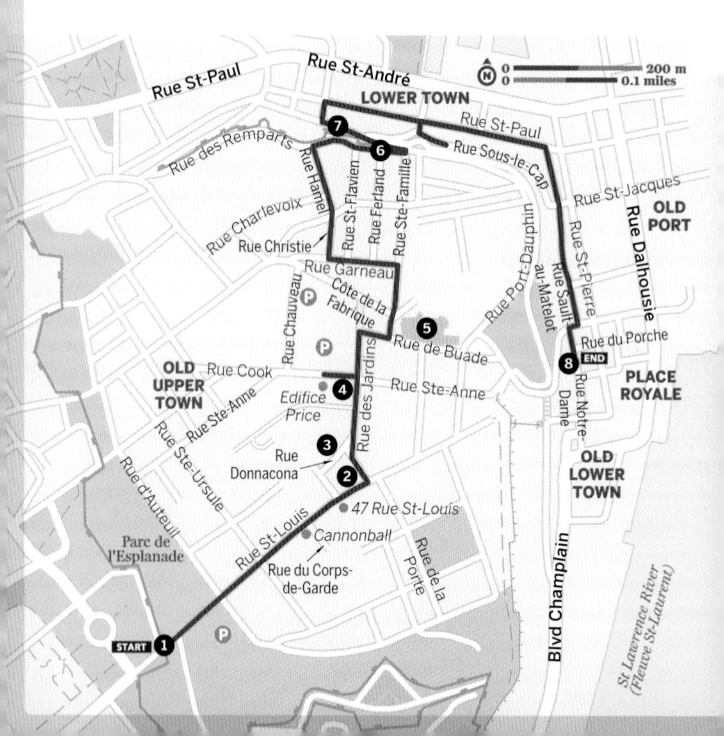

❶ Entry Gate

Begin at **Porte St-Louis**, an impressive gate first erected in 1693. Follow Rue St-Louis to the corner of Rue du Corps-de-Garde, where a cannonball sits embedded in a tree (allegedly since 1759). Further on at 47 Rue St-Louis is where French General Montcalm died after being shot by the British during the Battle of the Plains of Abraham.

❷ European Architecture

At 34 Rue St-Louis, a 1676 home houses the Québécois restaurant **Aux Anciens Canadiens** (p117). Its steeply pitched roof was typical of 17th-century French architecture.

❸ Nun Knowledge

Follow Rue des Jardins to the **Ursulines Chapel** (12 Rue Donnacona; 10:30am-noon & 1-4:30pm Tue-Sun May-Oct, 1-4:30pm Sat & Sun Nov-Apr) and museum where generations of nuns educated both French and Aboriginal girls from 1641.

❹ Art Deco Skyscraper

Left down Rue Ste-Anne is the elegant 1870 Hôtel Clarendon, Québec City's oldest hotel, currently undergoing renovations after a bad fire in January 2019. Next door is **Édifice Price** (www.ivanhoecambridge.com/en/office-buildings/properties/edifice-price; 65 Rue Ste-Anne), one of Canada's first skyscrapers, built in 1929 for $1 million. Enter for a look at the art-deco lobby.

❺ Cathedral & Prison

A short stroll along Rue des Jardins and Rue de Buade brings you to the heavily restored **Basilique-Cathédrale Notre-Dame-de-Québec** (418-694-0665; http://holydoorquebec.ca/en; 8:45am-3:45pm Mon-Fri, to 4:45pm Sat & Sun, to 8:15pm daily summer). To the left of the cathedral is the entrance to the Séminaire de Québec founded in 1663.

❻ Waterfront Views

Detour down pretty Rue Garneau, then descend to Rue des Remparts for fine views over the waterfront factory district.

❼ Descending to Lower Town

Descend Côte de la Canoterie, a historical link between the Lower and Upper Towns. Hope Gate stood atop the côte until 1873 to keep the riffraff from entering the Upper Town. Turn right at Rue St-Thomas and right again onto **Rue St-Paul** (M Place-d'Armes), the heart of Québec City's antiques district.

❽ Historical Mural

Turn right and follow pretty Rue Sault-au-Matelot to the 420-sq-meter trompe-l'oeil **Fresque des Québécois** (Québec City Mural; 29 Rue Notre-Dame, Parc de la Cetière), where you can pose alongside historical figures like Jacques Cartier and Samuel de Champlain.

Rue Dalhousie
Musée de la Civilisation
OLD PORT
PLACE ROYALE
Rue St-Antoine
Rue St-Pierre
Rue Sault-au-Matelot
Rue Notre-Dame
L'Oncle Antoine
Rue St-Jacques
Rue Prince de Galles
Pointe à Carcy
Bassin Louise
Rue Port-Dauphin
Côte de la Montagne
Frontenac Kiosk
Rue du Fort
Rue du Trésor
Rue des Jardins
Musée des Ursulines
OLD UPPER TOWN
Rue Ste-Anne
Rue Dauphine
Centre Infotouriste Québec City
Rue de Buade
5 Musée de l'Amérique Francophone
Artisans Canada
Côte de la Fabrique
Rue Garneau
Rue Chauveau
Rue Cook
Rue St-Stanislas
Rue Ste-Angèle
Rue St-Jean
Rue McMahon
Parc de l'Artillerie
Place d'Youville
Rue Richelieu
Côte du Palais
Rue Hébert
Rue Ste-Famille
Rue Couillard
Rue Charlevoix
Rue Hamel
1 Le Monastère des Augustines
Rue Sous-le-Cap
Côte de la Canoterie
Côte Dinan
Rue des Remparts
Rue St-Vallier Est
Rue des Prairies
Rue St-Nicholas
Rue St-Paul
LOWER TOWN
Rue St-André
Carré Parent
Ruelle Légaré
Quai St-André
Rue Abraham-Martin
Gare du Palais
0 200 m
0 0.1 miles
A B C D E F
1 2 3 4
6 7 10 11 12 15 16 17 18 20

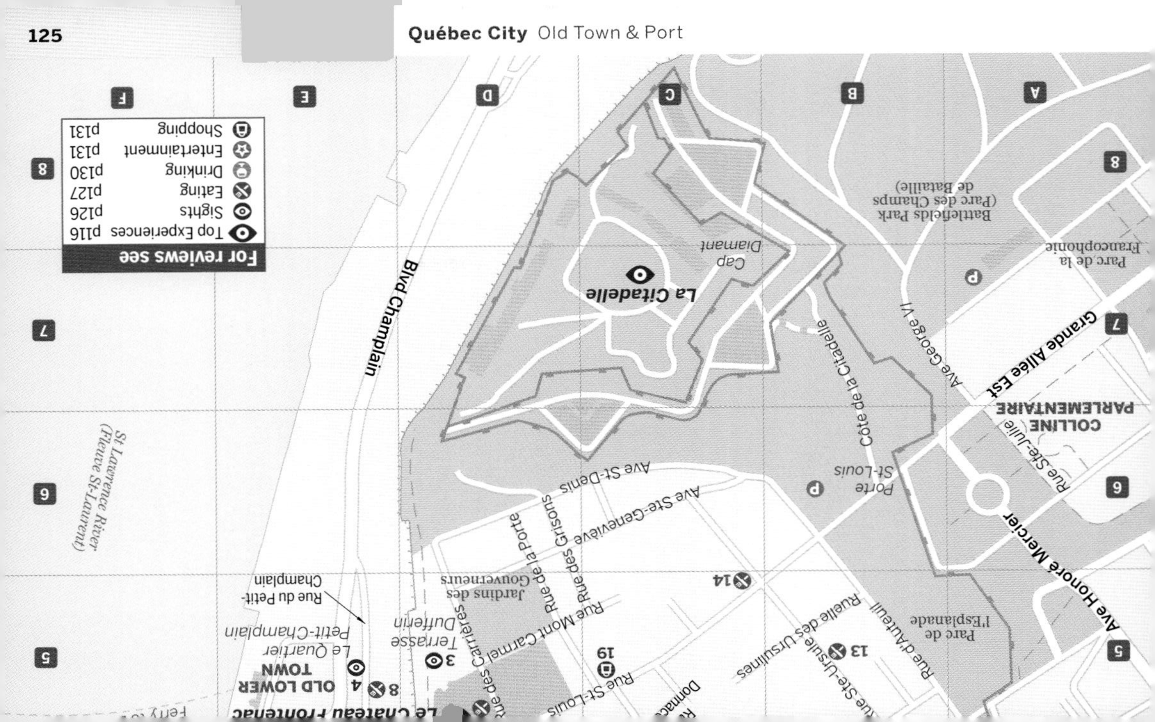

For reviews see
Top Experiences p116
Sights p126
Eating p127
Drinking p130
Entertainment p131
Shopping p131
La Citadelle
Cap Diamant
Blvd Champlain
St Lawrence River (Fleuve St-Laurent)
OLD LOWER TOWN
Le Quartier Petit-Champlain
Rue du Petit-Champlain
Terrasse Dufferin
Le Château Frontenac
Jardins des Gouverneurs
Rue des Carrières
Rue Mont Carmel
Rue de la Porte
Rue des Grisons
Ave Ste-Geneviève
Ave St-Denis
Rue St-Louis
Rue Ste-Ursule
Ruelle des Ursulines
Rue d'Auteuil
Parc de l'Esplanade
Porte St-Louis
Côte de la Citadelle
Ave George VI
Battlefields Park (Parc des Champs de Bataille)
Parc de la Francophonie
Grande Allée Est
COLLINE PARLEMENTAIRE
Rue Ste-Julie
Ave Honoré Mercier

Sights

Le Monastère des Augustines
MUSEUM

1 MAP P124, B2

On no account should you miss this museum, which traces the history of the order of Augustinian nuns who founded Québec's first hospital, the Hôtel-Dieu, in 1644 and ran it for over 300 years. OK, it may not sound like a crowd-pleaser, but the half dozen rooms around a central cloister are filled with remarkable displays of religious items, crafts (artificial flowers were mandatory where flowers bloom only four months a year), an old apothecary and an 18th-century refectory. (☎418-694-1639; https://monastere.ca; 77 Rue des Remparts; adult/youth/child $10.50/4.50/free, guided tour $15/9/free; 10am-5pm late Jun-Aug, Tue-Sun Sep-late Jun)

Musée des Ursulines
MUSEUM

2 MAP P124, C4

Housed in a historic convent, this thoughtful, well-laid-out and wheelchair-accessible museum tells the fascinating story of the Ursuline nuns' lives and their influence in the 17th and 18th centuries. The sisters established North America's first school for girls in 1641, educating both Aboriginal and French students. Displays on convent school life are enlivened by a vast array of historic artifacts, including examples of the Ursulines' gold and silver embroidery. (Ursulines Museum; ☎418-694-0694; www.poleculturedesursulines.ca; 10 Rue Donnacona; adult/youth/child $10/5/free; 10am-5pm Tue-Sun May-Sep, 1-5pm Tue-Sun Oct-Apr)

Terrasse Dufferin
PARK

3 MAP P124, D5

Perched on a clifftop 60m above the St Lawrence River, this 425m-long boardwalk is a marvelous setting for a stroll, with spectacular, sweeping views. In summer it's peppered with street performers; in winter it hosts a dramatic toboggan run (p18). Near the statue of Samuel de Champlain, stairways descend to the excavations of Champlain's **second fort** (☎418-648-7016; www.pc.gc.ca/en/lhn-nhs/qc/saintlouisforts; Terrasse Dufferin; adult/child $4/free, incl guided tour $15/10; 9am-5:30pm mid-May–early Oct), which stood here from 1620 to 1635. Nearby, you can take the funicular (p148) to the Old Lower Town. (Rue des Carrières)

Le Quartier Petit-Champlain
AREA

4 MAP P124, E5

Arguably the city's most picturesque district, this area sandwiched between the Old Upper Town and the waterfront has Québec City's most intriguing museums and galleries, plus numerous plaques and statues and plenty of outdoor cafes and restaurants along its pedestrian-friendly streets.

Musée de l'Amérique Francophone

MUSEUM

5 MAP P124, D3

Anchor tenant of the 17th-century **Séminaire de Québec** (Côte de la Fabrique), this breathtakingly thorough museum is purported to be Canada's oldest. Enter via the awesome Chapelle du Musée (Museum Chapel), built in 1898 by Joseph-Ferdinand Peachy, who earlier built the Église St-Jean-Baptiste. Access the main building pavilion by underground tunnel and its three floors of exhibits exploring the diaspora of French-speaking people in North America, the early years of New France and the work of artists and artisans here since 1930. (Museum of French-Speaking America; 418-643-2158, 866-710-8031; www.mcq.org/en/informations/maf; 2 Côte de la Fabrique; adult/teen/child $10/4/free; 10am-5pm mid-Jun–Aug, Sat & Sun Sep–mid-Jun)

Eating

Chez Temporel

CAFE $

6 MAP P124, C3

Hidden away on a side street just off the beaten path, this charming little cafe serves tasty sandwiches, homemade soups and quiches, pizza plus prodigious salads, fresh-baked goods and excellent coffee. Being slightly off the track, it attracts a healthy mix of locals and travelers. (418-694-1813;

Le Monastère des Augustines

L'Oncle Antoine

Set clandestinely in the vaulted brick cellar of one of the city's oldest surviving houses (dating from 1754), this great **tavern** (Map p124, E4; 418-694-9176; 29 Rue St-Pierre; 11am-1am) pours excellent Québec microbrews (try the Barberie Noir stout), several drafts and various European beers. Its in-house brews include #1 Blonde (lager), #21 Rousse (red) and #29 IPA. Try its famous onion soup on a cold Sunday afternoon.

www.facebook.com/cheztemporel; 25 Rue Couillard; mains $9-20; 11am-5pm Mon-Thu, to 8:30pm Fri & Sat, to 7:30pm Sun)

Paillard CAFE, BAKERY $

7 MAP P124, B4

At this bright, buzzy and high-ceilinged *café-boulangerie* (cafe-bakery) crammed with tourists, diners seated at long wooden tables tuck into tasty gourmet sandwiches, soups and salads. The attached bakery, with its alluring display cases, is downright irresistible – try the *tentation* ($3), a delicious sweet pastry loaded with berries. (418-692-1221; www.paillard.ca; 1097 Rue St-Jean; sandwiches $9-11; 7am-9pm Sun-Thu, to 10pm Fri & Sat)

Le Lapin Sauté FRENCH $$

8 MAP P124, E5

Naturally, *lapin* (rabbit) plays a starring role at this cozy, rustic restaurant just south of the funicular's lower terminus, in such dishes as rabbit cassoulet or rabbit poutine. Other enticements include salads, French onion soup, charcuterie platters and an excellent-value lunch menu (from $16). In good weather, sit on the flowery patio overlooking tiny Parc Félix-Leclerc. (418-692-5325; www.lapinsaute.com; 52 Rue du Petit-Champlain; mains $17-29; 11am-10pm Mon-Fri, 9am-10pm Sat & Sun)

1608 CHEESE $$

9 MAP P124, D5

At this Frontenac-based wine-and-cheese bar you can either select some cheeses yourself or let the staff take you down a wine-and-cheese rabbit hole that's difficult to emerge from; platters of three/four/five cheeses are $21/26/30 (five types with charcuterie $34). Wine, *fromage* and an incomparable view of the St Lawrence all make for a very romantic setting. (418-692-3861; http://1608baravin.com; 1 Rue des Carrières, Fairmount Le Château Frontenac; mains $21-34; 4pm-midnight Sun-Thu, 2pm-1am Fri & Sat)

Le Café du Monde BISTRO $$

10 MAP P124, F2

This Paris-style bistro is the only restaurant in town directly on the St Lawrence River, although actually getting a table with a view can sometimes be a challenge. Persevere. Bright, airy and casually elegant, it swears by bistro classics like *steak frites* (steak and fries) and duck confit, but there's also a great choice of other dishes, from grilled salmon to deer stew. (☎418-692-4455; www.lecafedumonde.com; 84 Rue Dalhousie; mains $20-33; ⏰11:30am-10pm Mon-Fri, from 9am Sat & Sun)

Légende

QUÉBÉCOIS **$$**

11 MAP P124, B2

Seasonal cuisine and fine-wine pairings are the name of the game at this classy restaurant under the direction of renowned restaurateurs Karen Therrien and Frédéric Laplante. Québécois oysters, mackerel, lamb and duck share the menu with artisanal cheeses and specialty ingredients such as balsamic-like birch syrup, chanterelle mushrooms and fiddlehead ferns. (☎418-614-2555; http://restaurantlegende.com/restaurant-legende-quebec; 255 Rue St-Paul; mains $19-24; ⏰5:30-10pm Wed-Sun)

Chez Boulay

QUÉBÉCOIS **$$$**

12 MAP P124, B3

Renowned chef Jean-Luc Boulay's flagship restaurant serves an ever-evolving menu inspired by seasonal Québécois staples such as venison, goose, blood pudding, wild mushrooms and Gaspé Peninsula seafood. Lunch specials and charcuterie platters for two (served 2pm to 5pm) offer an affordable

Le Lapin Sauté

afternoon pick-me-up, while the sleek, low-lit dining area with views of the open kitchen makes for a romantic dinner setting. (418-380-8166; www.chezboulay.com; 1110 Rue St-Jean; lunch menus $18-24, dinner mains $26-35; 11:30am-10pm Mon-Fri, 10am-10pm Sat & Sun)

Le St-Amour FRENCH, QUÉBÉCOIS $$$

13 MAP P124, B5

One of Québec City's top-end darlings, Le St-Amour has earned a loyal following because of its beautifully prepared grills and seafood, and its luxurious surroundings. The soaring greenhouse-style ceiling trimmed with hanging plants creates an inviting setting, and the midday *table d'hôte* ($18 to $33; available weekdays) offers that rarest of Upper Town experiences – a world-class meal at an extremely reasonable price. (418-694-0667; www.saint-amour.com; 48 Rue Ste-Ursule; mains $42-52, tasting menus $72 & $130; 11:30am-2pm Mon-Fri, 5:30-10pm daily)

Bello Ristorante ITALIAN $$$

14 MAP P124, C5

Luc Ste-Croix, former student of French master chef Paul Bocuse, brings his passion for Italian cuisine to this stylish and very welcoming eatery near Porte St-Louis. The vast menu ranges from wood-fired pizzas and scrumptious risottos to Parmesan veal scaloppini. Make sure you save some room at dessert-time for delicious tiramisu ($12), made the right way with real mascarpone. (418-694-0030; www.belloristorante.com; 73 Rue St-Louis; mains $17-38; 11:30am-11:30pm)

Drinking

Pub des Borgia BAR

15 MAP P124, E4

This hidden nook of a bar huddles by the cobblestones of Old Lower Town and, on the inside, seems to exemplify the colonial coziness that you'd expect of drinking establishments in this area. With that said, while the interior has a cellar-esque quality, the adjoining patio adds a bit of fresh air and allows for some Rue du Petit-Champlain people-watching. (581-300-9176; www.facebook.com/pubdesborgia; 12 Rue du Petit-Champlain; 11am-1am)

Bar Ste-Angèle BAR

16 MAP P124, B4

A low-lit and intimate hipster hangout, where the genial staff will help you to navigate the list of different cocktail pitchers and various local and European bottled craft beers. If you're lucky, you can enjoy live jazz, which is performed by both local and visiting musicians on selected nights. (418-692-2171; www.facebook.com/BarSainteAngele; 26 Rue Ste-Angèle; 8pm-3am)

Entertainment

Pape Georges

LIVE MUSIC

17 MAP P124, E4

With live music from 10pm on Friday and Saturday night at the very minimum (more in the summer), this charming bar located in a 400-year-old house also serves cheeses, meats and baguettes with a healthy dollop of Québécois culture. It always attracts a lively crowd. (418-692-1320; www.facebook.com/papegeorges; 8 Rue de Cul-de-Sac; 11am-3pm)

Bar Les Yeux Bleus

LIVE MUSIC

18 MAP P124, B3

One of the city's better *boîtes á chanson* (live, informal singer-songwriter clubs), this is the place to catch newcomers, the occasional big-name francophone concert and Québécois classics. It's in an old wooden house down a narrow alleyway from Rue St-Jean in the Old Upper Town. (418-694-9118; 1117 Rue St-Jean; 9pm-3am Mon, Tue & Thu, 8pm-3am Wed, 4pm-3am Fri-Sun, closed Mon-Wed winter)

Shopping

Galerie d'Art Inuit Brousseau

ART

19 MAP P124, C5

Devoted to Inuit soapstone, serpentine and basalt carvings and sculptures from artists all over Arctic Canada, this place is gorgeously set up and elaborately lit, with well-trained staff who knowledgeably answer questions. Works range from the small to the large and intricate. Expect high quality and steep prices. International shipping is available. (418-694-1828; www.artinuit.ca; 35 Rue St-Louis; 9:30am-5:30pm)

Artisans Canada

One of our favorite stores to shop and browse, this **emporium** (Map p124, C3; 888-339-2109, 418-692-2109; www.artisanscanada.com; 30 Côte de la Fabrique; 10am-7pm Sat-Thu, to 9pm Fri) run by the same family for three generations stocks arts and crafts, clothing, jewelry and quality souvenirs created by 100 different Québécois and Canadian artists. It also stocks the world-renowned Tilley hat, Canada's greatest contribution to the world of headgear.

Boutique Métiers d'Art du Québec

ARTS & CRAFTS

20 MAP P124, E4

Run by the organization that oversees all sorts of arts and crafts disciplines in Québec, this stylish boutique in the Place Royale sells the best of Québécois porcelain, ceramics, jewelry, wood carving and a lot of unusual (and fun) gifts. (418-694-0267, 418-694-0260; www.metiersdart.ca; 20 Rue Notre-Dame; 10am-6pm Mon-Sat, to 5pm Sun)

Explore

Outside the Old Town

It's well worth venturing outside the Old Town to visit sights like Battlefields Park and the Musée National des Beaux-Arts du Québec as well as architectural icons like the Hôtel du Parlement. Sightseeing aside, some of Québec City's best neighborhoods for strolling, dining and drinking are found here, including bohemian St-Jean Baptiste and the up-and-coming St-Roch.

The Short List

- **Battlefields Park (p139)** *Walking, cycling, cross-country skiing or celebrating Winter Carnival in the city's verdant oasis.*
- **Musée National des Beaux-Arts du Québec (p138)** *Discovering a staggering range of artistic treasures including Inuit works from more than 60 artists.*
- **Musée des Plaines d'Abraham (p139)** *Learning about the 18th-century battles that shaped Québec's history.*
- **Obsérvatoire de la Capitale (p142)** *Admiring the view from the 221m observatory.*
- **St-Jean Baptiste (p134)** *Taking in the passing street scene from a terrace cafe in one of Québec City's most vibrant neighborhoods.*

Getting There & Around

Bus 1 links the Old Lower Town and ferry terminal with St-Roch and St-Sauveur via train and bus stations.

Outside the Old Town Map on p136

Battlefields Park (p139)

Walking Tour

Hip Hop Through St-Jean Baptiste

This walk leads you through boho St-Jean Baptiste, one of Québec City's best districts for strolling, with excellent shops, restaurants and bars. You'll also take in grand churches and theaters, as well as vestiges from the old fortifications. St-Jean Baptiste's back lanes are packed with the clapboard houses so distinctive of Québec City.

Walk Facts

Start Porte St-Jean; 🚌 11

End Ascenseur du Faubourg; 🚌 1

Length 3km; two hours

❶ Center for the Arts

Begin at **Porte St-Jean**, northernmost of the Old City's three main town gates originally built in 1693. Further along Rue St-Jean on the left is the renovated **Théâtre Capitole** (p15), the city's first theater, which opened as the Auditorium de Québec in 1903.

❷ Photogenic Chapel

Turn right at Rue d'Youville and follow it to the Convent of the Sisters of Charity and its magnificent galleried chapel.

❸ Bibles into Books

At the corner with Rue St-Jean is the onetime Anglican **Church of St Matthew** (418-641-6798; www.bibliothequedequebec.qc.ca/bibliotheques/lacitelimoilou/claire_martin.aspx; 755 Rue St-Jean; 10am-5pm Fri-Tue, 1-8pm Wed & Thu), transformed into a public library in 1980. The adjoining cemetery, which functioned as a Protestant burial ground from 1772 until 1860, is now the Parc St-Matthew.

❹ Historic Grocery

One block along Rue St-Jean is **JA Moisan Épicier** (418-522-0685; www.jamoisan.com; 695 Rue St-Jean; 8:30am-7pm Mon-Wed & Sat, to 9pm Thu & Fri, 10am-7pm Sun, extended hours summer), the oldest grocery store (1871) in North America.

❺ Architectural Gem

At the corner of Rue Ste-Claire is the colossal Second Empire–style **Église St-Jean-Baptiste** (www.saintjeanbaptiste.org; 470 Rue St-Jean), rebuilt in 1884 after a devastating fire three years before. Around the church are some colorful wooden clapboard houses rebuilt after the fires of 1845 and 1881.

❻ Theatrical Synagogue

Near the corner with Ave de Salaberry is the **Théâtre Périscope** (418-529-2183; www.theatreperiscope.qc.ca; 2 Rue Crémazie Est). Go around the front to see its previous incarnation – the Hebrew letters identify it as the synagogue Beth Israel Ohev Sholom.

❼ Old Fortifications

At Rue Philippe-Dorval, turn left and walk north to Martello Tower 4, one of three such fortifications in town. You can descend steps here but you'll probably prefer continuing east along Rue St-Réal to the **Ascenseur du Faubourg** (Suburban Elevator; Rue St-Réal; 7am-7pm Mon-Wed, to 10pm Thu & Fri, 10am-10pm Sat, to 7pm Sun), an elevator that will take you down to the district of St-Roch.

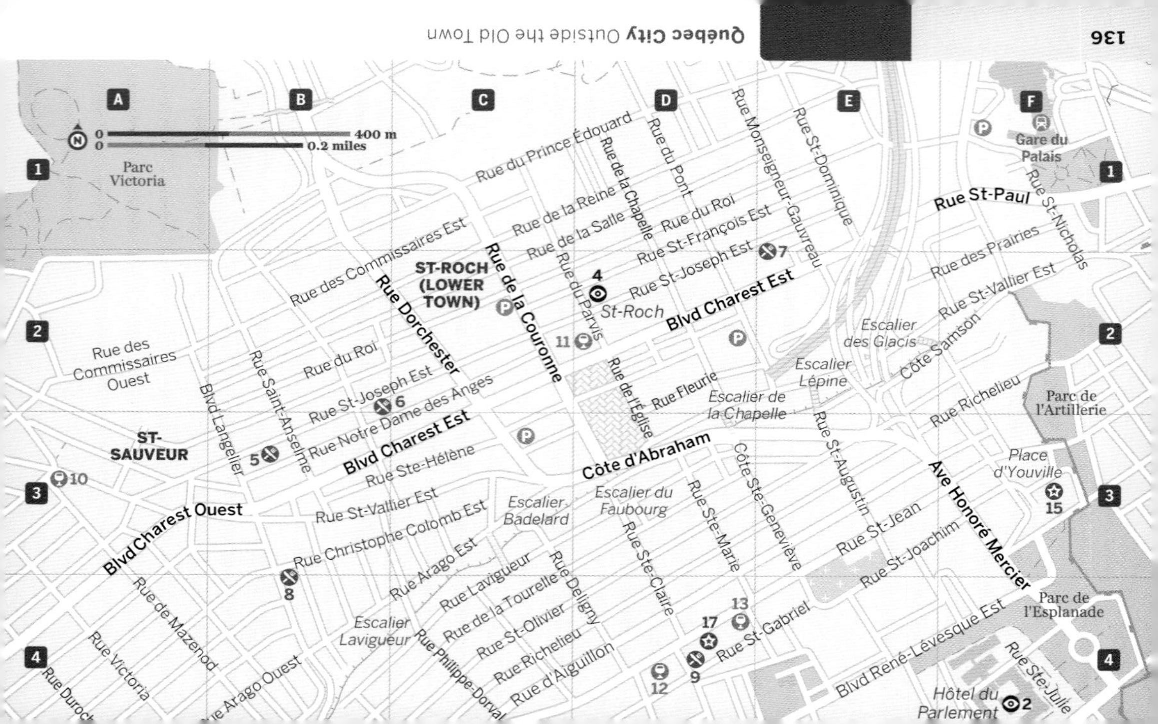
A
B
C
D
E
F
1
2
3
4
0
400 m
0
0.2 miles
Parc Victoria
Rue des Commissaires Ouest
ST-SAUVEUR
Blvd Charest Ouest
Blvd Langelier
Rue Saint-Anselme
Rue de Mazenod
Rue Victoria
Rue Duroc
Arago Ouest
Rue des Commissaires Est
Rue du Roi
Rue St-Joseph Est
Rue Notre Dame des Anges
Blvd Charest Est
Rue Ste-Hélène
Rue St-Vallier Est
Rue Christophe Colomb Est
Rue Arago Est
Rue Lavigueur
Escalier Lavigueur
Rue Philippe-Dorval
Rue Dorchester
ST-ROCH (LOWER TOWN)
Rue de la Couronne
Rue du Prince Édouard
Rue de la Reine
Rue de la Salle
Rue du Parvis
St-Roch
Escalier Badelard
Rue Deligny
Rue de la Tourelle
Rue St-Olivier
Rue Richelieu
Rue d'Aiguillon
Côte d'Abraham
Escalier du Faubourg
Rue Ste-Claire
Rue de l'Église
Rue de la Chapelle
Rue du Pont
Rue du Roi
Rue St-François Est
Rue St-Joseph Est
Blvd Charest Est
Rue Fleurie
Escalier de la Chapelle
Côte Ste-Geneviève
Rue Ste-Marie
Rue St-Gabriel
Rue Monseigneur-Gauvreau
Rue St-Dominique
Escalier Lépine
Escalier des Glacis
Rue St-Augustin
Rue St-Jean
Rue St-Joachim
Blvd René-Lévesque Est
Côte Samson
Rue St-Vallier Est
Rue des Prairies
Rue St-Paul
Rue St-Nicholas
Gare du Palais
Parc de l'Artillerie
Rue Richelieu
Place d'Youville
Ave Honoré Mercier
Parc de l'Esplanade
Rue Ste-Julie
Hôtel du Parlement
2
4
5
6
7
8
9
10
11
12
13
15
17

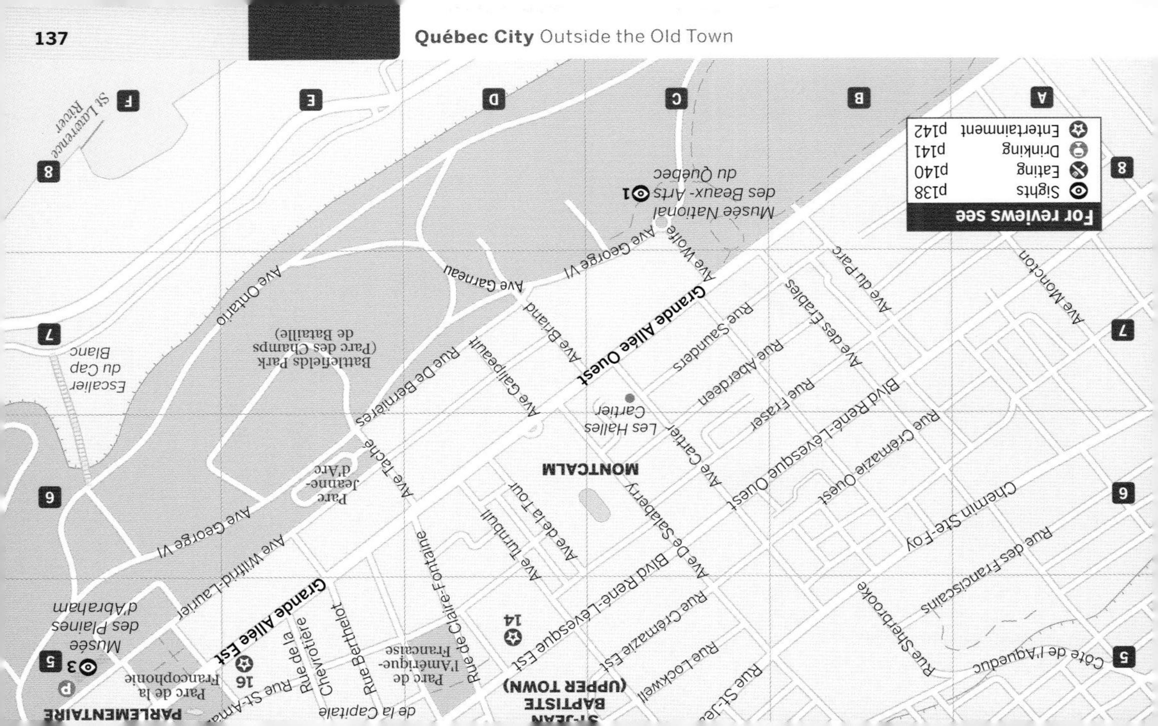
For reviews see
Sights p138
Eating p140
Drinking p141
Entertainment p142
A
B
C
D
E
F
5
6
7
8
St Lawrence River
Escalier du Cap Blanc
Battlefields Park (Parc des Champs de Bataille)
Parc Jeanne-d'Arc
Musée des Plaines d'Abraham
Musée National des Beaux-Arts du Québec
1
3
14
16
PARLEMENTAIRE
Parc de la Francophonie
Parc de l'Amérique-Française
ST-JEAN BAPTISTE (UPPER TOWN)
MONTCALM
Les Halles Cartier
Grande Allée Est
Grande Allée Ouest
Ave Ontario
Ave George VI
Ave Garneau
Ave Wolfe
Ave Wilfrid-Laurier
Rue De Bernières
Ave Taché
Ave Galipeault
Ave Briand
Rue Saunders
Rue Aberdeen
Rue Fraser
Ave des Érables
Ave du Parc
Ave Moncton
Blvd René-Lévesque Ouest
Rue Crémazie Ouest
Chemin Ste-Foy
Rue des Franciscains
Rue Sherbrooke
Côte de l'Aqueduc
Ave Cartier
Ave De Salaberry
Ave de la Tour
Ave Turnbull
Rue de Claire-Fontaine
Blvd René-Lévesque Est
Rue Crémazie Est
Rue Lockwell
Rue Berthelot
Rue de la Chevrotière
de la Capitale

Sights

Musée National des Beaux-Arts du Québec MUSEUM

1 MAP P136, C8

Spare at least a half-day to visit this extraordinary art museum, one of the province's best. Permanent exhibitions range from art in the early French colonies to Québec's contemporary artists, with individual halls devoted entirely to 20th-century artistic giants such as Jean-Paul Lemieux, Fernand Leduc and Jean-Paul Riopelle. Arguably the museum's highlight is the Brousseau Collection of Inuit Art, a selection of 100 pieces by 60 artists located at the top of the **Pavillon Pierre Lassonde**. (Québec National Museum of Fine Arts; 418-643-2150; www.mnbaq.org; 179 Grande Allée Ouest; adult/youth/child $20/11/free; 10am-6pm Jun-Aug, to 5pm Tue-Sun Sep-May, to 9pm Wed year-round)

Hôtel du Parlement HISTORIC BUILDING

2 MAP P136, F4

Home to Québec's Provincial Legislature, the gargantuan Parliament building is a Second Empire structure completed in 1886. Free 30-minute tours, offered in English and French, get you into the National Assembly Chamber, Legislative Council Chamber and President's Gallery. The facade is decorated with 26 statues, mostly of significant

Hôtel du Parlement

provincial historical figures, including explorer Samuel de Champlain (1570–1635), New France governor Louis de Buade Frontenac (1622–98) and English and French generals James Wolfe (1727–59) and Louis-Joseph Montcalm (1712–59). (Parliament Building; ☎418-643-7239; www.assnat.qc.ca/en/visiteurs; 1045 Rue des Parlementaires, enter from Grande Allée Est; admission free; ⊙8:30am-4:30pm Mon-Fri, 9:30am-4:30pm Sat & Sun late Jun-Aug, 8am-5pm Mon-Fri Sep-late Jun)

Musée des Plaines d'Abraham MUSEUM

3 MAP P136, F5

This museum spread over three levels presents a fine multimedia history show entitled *Battles: 1759–60*. Incorporating maps, scale models, interactive games, period uniforms and an overly long audiovisual presentation, the exhibit immerses visitors in the pivotal 18th-century battles that shaped Québec's destiny during the Seven Years' War between France and England. The experience is enlivened by first-hand accounts from the French, British, Canadian and Amerindian protagonists of the period. (Plains of Abraham Museum; ☎418-649-6157; www.theplainsofabraham.ca; 835 Ave Wilfrid-Laurier; adult/youth/child $12.25/10.25/4, incl Abraham's bus tour & Martello Tower 1 Jul-early Sep $15.25/11.25/5; ⊙9am-5:30pm)

Battlefields Park

One of Québec City's must-sees, this verdant clifftop **park** (Parc des Champs-de-Bataille; ☎418-649-6157; www.theplainsofabraham.ca; Ave George VI; ⊙9am-5:30pm; 👪) contains the Plains of Abraham, site of the infamous 1759 battle between British General James Wolfe and French General Louis-Joseph Montcalm that determined the fate of the North American continent. Packed with old cannons, monuments and Martello towers, it's a favorite local spot for picnicking, running, skating, skiing and snowshoeing, along with Winter Carnival festivities and open-air summer concerts.

St-Roch AREA

4 MAP P136, D2

Traditionally a working-class district for factory and navy employees, St-Roch has been slowly gentrifying over the past decade or so. On the main artery, Rue St-Joseph, spiffy restaurants and bars have sprung up among the junk shops and secondhand clothing stores. Private art galleries are also found here and along Rue St-Vallier Est. Walking down Côte Ste-Geneviève in St-Jean Baptiste, you will come to a steep staircase called Escalier de la

Chapelle, which will take you down to St-Roch.

Eating

Tora-Ya Ramen

JAPANESE $

5 MAP P136, B3

Catering to a young, informal clientele, this straight-ahead noodle house specializes in delicious ramen soups filled with pork, fish, tofu and loads of veggies. Draft beer, wine and a good sake selection make it a cozy place for a sit-down meal, but it's also a great takeout option if you'd rather hunker down in your hotel for a night. (418-780-1903; www.torayaramen.com; 75 Rue St-Joseph Est; mains $12-15; 11:30am-2pm Tue-Fri, 5-10pm Tue-Sat)

St-Roch (p139)

Le Croquembouche

BAKERY $

6 MAP P136, B2

Widely hailed as Québec City's finest bakery, Le Croquembouche draws devoted locals from dawn to dusk. Among its seductive offerings are fluffy-as-cloud croissants, tantalizing cakes and éclairs, brioches brimming with raspberries, and gourmet sandwiches on fresh-baked bread. There's also a stellar array of *danoises* (Danish pastries), including orange and anise, cranberry, pistachio and chocolate. (418-523-9009; www.lecroquembouche.com; 225 Rue St-Joseph Est; pastries from $2, sandwiches from $5.25; 7am-6:30pm Tue-Sat, to 5pm Sun;)

Poutineville

QUÉBÉCOIS $

7 MAP P136, E1

This could be the place for poutine virgins to try what has become the Québécois national dish – french fries served with cheese curds and swimming in gravy. But don't stop at just the garden-variety poutine: this is *la poutine réinventée*, where you'll find such additions as hot dogs, smoked meat, feta cheese or Mexican chili. (581-981-8188; www.poutineville.com; 735 Rue St-Joseph Est; mains $12-16; 11am-10pm Sun-Wed, to 11pm Thu, to midnight Fri & Sat)

Battuto

ITALIAN $$

8 MAP P136, B4

Considered by many Québécois to be the best Italian restaurant in town, this wonderful place on the edge of St-Roch mixes traditional dishes like *vitello tonnato* (veal topped with a tuna sauce) with more inventive pasta ones such as Sicilian *casarecce* served with sweetbreads and sherry. It's a tiny place, with a mere 24 seats, so book well ahead. (☎418-614-4414; www.battuto.ca; 527 Blvd Langelier; mains $21-23; ⏰5:30-10pm Tue-Sat)

Buvette Scott FRENCH $$

At this tiny wine bistro with just eight tables and seating at the bar, enlightened French classics like breaded calf's brains, bone marrow and *brandade de morue* (Provençal puree of cod mixed with milk, olive oil and garlic and served with croutons) dominate the menu. The chalkboard wine list is exceptional, with six reds and six whites. (☎581-741-4464; www.buvettescott.com; 821 Rue Scott; mains $12-18; ⏰4:30-11pm Mon-Sat)

Drinking

Griendel Brasserie Artisanale MICROBREWERY

Anchor tenant on Rue St-Vallier Ouest in up-and-coming St-Sauveur, Griendel occupies a huge old corner shop with lots of windows and great light. Choose from among the two-dozen *broues* (brews) on the blackboard, most of which are brewed inhouse. There

Les Halles Cartier

Montcalm's very popular and somewhat pricey indoor food **market** (Map p136, C7; www.hallesdupetitquartier.com; 1191 Ave Cartier; ⏰7am-9pm Mon-Fri, to 7pm Sat & Sun) features individual stalls for bakers, chocolatiers, and fruit, vegetable, cheese, meat and fish vendors, plus a number of cafes and restaurants on two levels. It's sometimes referred to by its old name of Les Halles du Petit-Quartier.

are burgers and poutine, but it's generally agreed they serve the best fish 'n' chips ($15) in town. (☎591-742-2884; www.facebook.com/Brasserie.artisanale.griendel; 195 Rue St-Vallier Ouest; ⏰3pm-1am Mon-Wed, to 3am Thu & Fri, 1pm-3am Sat, to 1am Sun)

Noctem Artisans Brasseurs MICROBREWERY

11 MAP P136, D2

One of the most interesting microbreweries in town, Noctem goes beyond the *blonde* (lager), *blanche* (white), *rousse* (red) and IPA tick list to offer a blackboard of up to 18 different beers and ales that change daily. If peckish, eschew the pizza/burger/taco choices in favor of a platter of charcuterie to share. (☎581-742-7979; www.noctem.ca; 438 Rue du Parvis; ⏰11am-3am)

Le Sacrilège

BAR

12 MAP P136, D4

With its unmistakable sign of a laughing, dancing monk, this bar has long been the watering hole of choice for Québec's night owls. Even on Monday, it's standing-room only. There's a quite good selection of beers (including many craft varieties), live music most nights at 8pm and seating on a lovely garden terrace out back. (418-649-1985; www.lesacrilege.com; 447 Rue St-Jean; noon-3am)

Le Moine Échanson

WINE BAR

13 MAP P136, D4

A darling of the city's wine connoisseurs, this convivial brick-walled wine bar and bistro pours an ever-changing array of wines from all over the Mediterranean accompanied by hearty and homespun snacks and main dishes. Three-/four-course set menus are $40/45. (418-524-7832; www.lemoineechanson.com; 585 Rue St-Jean; 4-10pm Sun-Wed, to 11pm Thu-Sat)

Obsérvatoire de la Capitale

Head 221m up to the 31st floor of the **Édifice Marie-Guyart** (Capital Observatory; 418-644-9841, 888-497-4322; www.observatoire-capitale.org; 1037 Rue de la Chevrotière; adult/student/child $14.75/11.50/5; 10am-5pm Feb–mid-Oct, Tue-Sun mid-Oct–Jan) for great views of the Old Town, the St Lawrence River and (if it's clear) even the distant Laurentians. The information panels along the way will get you up to speed on some of the local history, city superlatives and 'fun facts.'

Entertainment

Grand Théâtre de Québec

PERFORMING ARTS

14 MAP P136, D5

Designed by the Polish-Canadian architect Victor Prus in 1971, the 'Great Theater' is Québec City's main performing-arts center, with a steady diet of top-quality classical concerts, opera, dance and theater. Major companies that are based or perform here regularly include the **Opéra de Québec** (418-529-0688; www.operadequebec.com; 1220 Ave Taché; 9am-noon & 1:30-5pm Mon-Fri), the **Orchestre Symphonique de Québec** (418-643-8131; www.osq.org; 269 Blvd René-Lévesque Est; box office noon-5pm Mon-Sat & 30min before performances) and the **Théâtre du Trident.** (418-643-8131, 418-643-5873; www.letrident.com; 269 Blvd René-Lévesque Est; box office 9am-noon & 1:30-4:30pm Mon-Thu). (877-643-8131, 418-643-8131; www.grandtheatre.qc.ca; 269 Blvd René-Lévesque Est; box office noon-5pm Mon-Sat & 30min before performances)

Palais Montcalm

LIVE MUSIC

15 MAP P136, F3

Just outside the walls of the Old Upper Town, this art-deco theater

HEMIS/ALAMY STOCK PHOTO ©

Le Sacrilège

hosts a stellar lineup of concerts year-round, featuring everything from chamber music to rock. The main performance space is renowned for its 'near perfect' acoustics. (877-641-6040, 418-641-6040; www.palaismontcalm.ca; 995 Place d'Youville; box office noon-6pm Mon-Fri, to 5pm Sat)

Les Voûtes de Napoléon

LIVE MUSIC

16 MAP P136, E5

At this jubilant *boîte à chanson* (folk-music club), it will likely be just you and the locals. There's lively Québécois music nightly, usually of the 'singer-with-guitar' variety, with lesser-known up-and-coming acts featuring prominently. You'll find 'Napoleon's Vaults' in an atmospheric old cellar with ancient arched stone walls just west of the Hôtel du Parlement (p138). (418-640-9388; www.voutesdenapoleon.com; 680a Grande Allée Est; 9:30pm-3am)

Fou-Bar

LIVE MUSIC

17 MAP P136, D4

Laid-back and offering an eclectic mix of bands, this bar is one of the town's classics for live music. It's also popular for its reasonably priced food menu and its free appetizers on Thursday and Friday evenings. There can be a cover charge of up to $20 depending on the band. (418-522-1987; www.foubar.ca; 525 Rue St-Jean; 2:30pm-1am Sun & Mon, to 2am Tue & Wed, to 3am Thu-Sat)

Survival Guide

Le Château Frontenac (p118) CHRISTOPHER BABCOCK/SHUTTERSTOCK ©

Before You Go

Book Your Stay

- French- and Victorian-style inns and independent hotels cater to a variety of budgets.
- Reserve at least a month in advance, especially from June to September, or for budget accommodations.
- Outside of high season summer months and during big events you can usually save 30% off the high-season prices.

Useful Websites

- **Lonely Planet** (lonelyplanet.com/canada/montreal/hotels) Recommendations and reviews.
- **BBCanada** (www.bbcanada.com) B&Bs in Montréal and beyond.
- **Tourisme Montréal** (www.mtl.org) Extensive listings from the city's tourism authority.
- **Tourisme Québec** (www.bonjourquebec.com) Lodging options from Québec City's official tourism board.

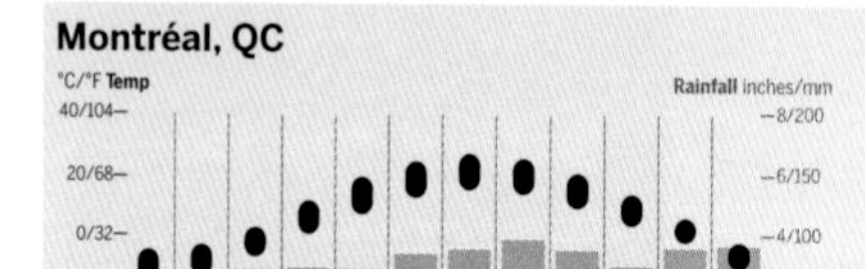

When to Go

- **Spring** April and May can be chilly, but there's excitement in the air as gardens bloom.
- **Summer** The liveliest time to visit is June through early September, with a busy events calendar, and long sunny days.
- **Fall** Pleasant weather and changing leaves make a pretty backdrop from mid September through October
- **Winter** Despite iciness, December to March offers rewarding festivals, snow sports and cultural fare.

Best Budget

- **Auberge St-Paul** (www.aubergesaintpaul.com) Friendly neat hostel in a great Old Montréal location.
- **Le Gîte du Plateau Mont-Royal** (www.hostelmontreal.com) Top pick with a rooftop terrace and location near Montréal's 'mountain'.

Best Midrange

- **Accueil Chez François** (www.chezfrancois.ca) Delicious breakfasts, friendly hosts and good-value rooms in Montréal.
- **Auberge De La Fontaine** (www.aubergedelafontaine.com) Based in Montréal's Plateau district, featuring suites with in-room spas and park views.

Best Top End

- **Hôtel Le St-James** Refined opulence in a 19th-century building in Old Montréal.
- **Hôtel Nelligan** (https://hotelnelligan.com) Two restored buildings shine with modern plush luxury and a great roof patio in Old Montréal.

Arriving in Montréal

Montréal-Pierre Elliott Trudeau International Airport

- Montréal is served by **Montréal-Pierre Elliott Trudeau International Airport,** (Trudeau, YUL; www.admtl.com) located 21km west of Downtown.
- **Bus** No 747 ($10) takes 25 to 60 minutes to get into town, dropping passengers Downtown, at St Lionel-Groulx metro station, then on to **Gare d'Autocars** (Map p70; ☎514-842-2281; www.gamtl.com; 1717 Rue Berri; Ⓜ Berri-UQAM) and Berri-UQAM metro station, in the Quartier Latin.
- **Taxi** It takes at least 20 minutes to get Downtown from the airport and the fixed fare is $40.

Gare Centrale

- Conveniently located **Gare Centrale** (Central Train Station; www.viarail.ca; 895 Rue de la Gauchetière Ouest; Ⓜ Bonaventure) is the local hub of VIA Rail, Canada's vast rail network, linking Montréal with cities across the country. It connects to the Bonaventure metro station.

Gare d'Autocars de Montréal

- Most long-distance buses arrive at Montréal's **Gare d'Autocars** (Map p70; ☎514-842-2281; www.gamtl.com; 1717 Rue Berri; Ⓜ Berri-UQAM), which is steps from the Berri-UQAM metro station.

Arriving in Québec City

Aéroport International Jean-Lesage de Québec

- Québec City's petite **Aéroport International Jean-Lesage de Québec** (YQB; ☎877-769-2700, 418-640-3300; www.aeroportdequebec.com; 505 Rue Principal) lies about 15km west of the Old Town.
- **Bus** No 76 goes from the airport to the train station, from where you change to city bus 11 to the Old Town; the entire trip takes nearly 2 hours.
- **Taxi** Costs a flat fee of just over $35 to go into the city and takes about 30 minutes.

Gare du Palais & Gare Routière de Québec

- Québec City's train station, **Gare du Palais** (Palace Station; ☎888-842-7245; www.viarail.ca; 450 Rue de la Gare du Palais), has four to six trains daily to/from Montréal (3¼-hour journey, from $42/87 one-way/return).
- **Bus** From the train station (also the city's bus station) catch bus 1 to the Old Lower Town, ferry terminal, St-Roch or St-Sauveur.
- **Foot** It's less than a 20-minute walk (about 1.2km) to the heart of the Old Town.

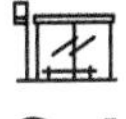

Getting Around

Montréal Metro

- **STM** (Société de Transport de Montréal; ☎514-786-4636; www.stm.info) is Montréal's metro (subway) and bus operator.

- Trains generally run from 5:30am to midnight from Sunday to Friday, slightly later on Saturday night (to 1:30am at the latest).
- A single bus or metro ticket costs $3.50 – and allows transfers between bus and metro.
- If you're sticking around Montréal for longer, rechargeable Opus cards cost $6 up front, but can be re-charged at a discounted rate for 10 rides ($30), one day of unlimited rides ($10, actually 24 hours), three days ($20.50), a week ($28) or a month ($90.50).

Québec City Buses

- The most convenient hub for catching multiple buses is on Place d'Youville, just outside the Old Town walls.
- Bus No 1 Links the Old Lower Town and ferry terminal with St-Roch and St-Sauveur via the Gare du Palais train and bus stations.
- Bus No 11 Links Montcalm and Colline Parlementaire with the Old Upper Town (the only bus running here).

Bicycle

- Montréal has over 500km of paths around the city. Québec City has around 70km of bike paths, including a route along the St Lawrence that connects to paths along the Rivière St-Charles.
- Montréal's public bike-rental service **Bixi** (514-789-2494; http://montreal.bixi.com; per 30min $2.95; 24hr mid-Apr–Oct) is easy to use and has over 500 rental stations around town.
- In Québec City, **Cyclo Services** (418-692-4052, 877-692-4050; www.cycloservices.net; 289 Rue St-Paul; rental per 2/24hr city bike $17/38, electric bike $34/76; 9am-5:30pm Mon-Fri, 10am-5pm Sat & Sun, variable hours Nov-Apr;), just across from the Gare du Palais (train station), rents a wide variety of bikes.

Taxi & Ride Share

Flag fall in both Montréal and Québec City is a standard $3.50, plus another $1.70 per kilometer and 65¢ per minute spent waiting in traffic. Uber is available in both Montréal and Québec City.

Funicular

Funicular (www.funiculaire-quebec.com; Rue du Petit-Champlain; one way $3.50; 7:30am-10:30pm, to 11:30pm summer) links the Old Upper and Lower Towns of Québec City.

Essential Information

Accessible Travel

- Most public buildings in Montréal and Québec City – including tourist offices, major museums and attractions – are accessible for people in wheelchairs. Many restaurants and hotels have facilities for the mobility-impaired but not in the old parts of town (Old Montréal and Québec City's Old Town), where very few buildings have elevators.
- In Montréal, the public transport system is quite accessibility friendly, provided weather conditions permit. Check the STM page (www.stm.info/en/access).

- In Québec City, RTC city bus line 11 and high-frequency Métrobus lines 800, 801, 802, 803, 804 and 807 are wheelchair accessible. The 'Accessibility' section of the RTC website (www.rtcquebec.ca) has more details.
- Featured accessible accommodation is searchable on Québec For All (http://quebecforall.com).

Business Hours

Banks 10am–3pm Monday to Friday (later on Thursday).

Bars & Pubs 11:30am–midnight or later; those not serving food may not open until 5pm or later.

Museums 10am or 11am to 6pm. Most close Monday, but open late one day a week.

Restaurants 11:30am–2:30pm and 5:30pm–11pm; cafes serving breakfast open 7am –9am.

Discount Cards

The **Montréal Museum Pass** (www.museesmontreal.org) allows free access to 39 museums for any three days in a 21-day period ($80). It comes with three consecutive days of free access to bus and metro. It's available from tourist offices, major museums, or online.

Electricity

Type A
120V/60Hz

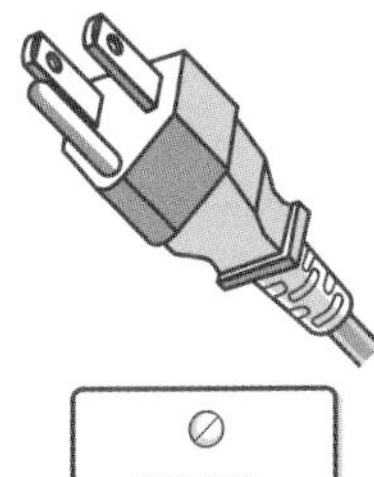

Type B
120V/60Hz

Emergencies

Call **911** for ambulance, fire or police.

LGBTIQ+ Travelers

- Montréal is popular with lesbian, gay and bisexual travelers. The gay community is centered in The Village. The weeklong **Montréal Pride** (Fierté Montréal; 514-903-6193; http://fiertemtl.com; Aug) attracts hundreds of thousands every August, while the **Black & Blue Festival** (514-875-7026; www.bbcm.org; Oct) in early October features major dance parties and cultural and arts events.
- Québec City's gay community is tiny but well established, with its own Pride festival, the Fête Arc-en-Ciel in September, and a handful of popular nightspots along Rue St-Jean in St-Jean Baptiste.
- Fugues (www.fugues.com) is a free gay and lesbian entertainment guide with listings for Québec.

Money

Credit cards are widely accepted.

ATMs Montréal and Québec City have many

ATMs linked to the international Cirrus, Plus and Maestro networks. Most charge a small fee, though Banque Nationale charges no usage fees for some cards.

Tipping 15% of the pretax bill is customary in restaurants.

Changing Money Aside from banks, there are foreign-exchange desks at Montréal's main tourist office, the airport and the casino.

Public Holidays

New Year's Day January 1

Good Friday & Easter Monday Late March to mid-April

Victoria Day May 24 or nearest Monday

National Aboriginal Day June 21 (unofficial)

St-Jean-Baptiste Day June 24

Canada Day July 1

Labour Day First Monday in September

Canadian Thanksgiving Second Monday in October

Remembrance Day November 11

Christmas Day December 25

Boxing Day December 26

Safe Travel

- Violent crime is rare (especially involving foreigners). Even so, as in any city, it's best to stay alert for petty theft and use hotel safes where available.
- Cars with foreign registration are occasionally targeted for smash-and-grab theft. Don't leave valuables in the car.
- Take special care at pedestrian crosswalks: unless there's an *arrêt* (stop) sign, drivers largely ignore these crosswalks.
- Québec's COVID-19 guidance for visitors has evolved over time. For the latest information on visiting Montréal, see www.mtl.org/en/covid-19; and for Québec City, see www.quebec-cite.com/en/about/coronavirus.

Telephone Services

- The area code for the entire island of Montréal is 514. The area code for Québec City is 418 (and occasionally 581).
- The only foreign cell phones that will work in North America are triband models operating on GSM 1900. If you don't have one of these, your best bet is to buy an inexpensive phone with prepaid minutes and a rechargeable SIM card at a consumer electronics store such as the chain Best Buy (www.bestbuy.ca).
- US residents traveling with their phone may have service (though they may have to pay roaming fees). Get in touch with your cell-phone provider for details.

Toilets

Public sit-down toilets are plentiful in busy areas and at all metro stations. They are always free to use.

Tourist Information

Centre Infotouriste Montréal (Map p56; 514-844-5400; www.mtl.org; 1255 Rue Peel; 9am-6pm May-Sep, to 5pm Oct-Apr; M Peel) provides maps, info about attractions and booking services.

Tourisme Montréal (877-266-5687; www.mtl.org; 9am-noon & 1-5pm Mon-Fri, from 10am Wed) Has reams of information and a last-minute hotel search

Money-Saving Tips

- Make lunch (called dîner here) your main meal. Many restaurants offer midday *table d'hôtes* (fixed-price menus) for about half the price of a comparable evening meal.
- Many pubs and bars offer generous *cinq-à-sept* (5pm to 7pm) happy-hour prices, particularly on Thursdays and Fridays.
- Sightsee on foot. Walking is one of the best ways to get around the main areas of Montréal and Québec City – it's quick, cheap and you'll see a lot more than you would by public transportation.

engine with guaranteed best price.

Centre Infotouriste Québec City (Québec Original; Map p124; ☎418-641-6290, 877-266-5687; www.quebecoriginal.com; 12 Rue Ste-Anne; ⏰9am-5pm Nov-Jun, to 6pm Jul-Oct) The main tourist office, in the heart of the Old Town. It has scads of brochures and maps, and helpful staff.

Frontenac Kiosk (Map p124; www.pc.gc.ca/eng/lhn-nhs/qc/fortifications; off Rue St-Louis; adult/child $4/free; ⏰10am-5pm mid-May–early Oct, to 6pm Jul & Aug) In summer, this Québec City kiosk offers tourist information for (and entry to) the Fortifications of Québec and St-Louis Forts & Châteaux national historic sites.

Musée des Plaines d'Abraham (Plains of Abraham Museum; Map p136; www.theplainsofabraham.ca; 835 Ave Wilfrid-Laurier; adult/youth/child $12.25/10.25/4, incl Abraham's bus tour & Martello Tower 1 Jul-early Sep $15.25/11.25/5; ⏰9am-5:30pm) Reception in the museum's lower-ground floor provides information on the Plains of Abraham and Battlefields Park in Québec City.

Visas

- Citizens of dozens of countries – including the USA, most Western European countries, Australia, Japan, Taiwan, Mexico and New Zealand – don't need visas to enter Canada for stays of up to 180 days. US permanent residents are also exempt.
- You need an Electronic Travel Authorization (eTA) to fly into Canada. The eTA costs $7 and you can apply online at https://www.canada.ca/en/immigration-refugees-citizenship/services/visit-canada/eta/apply.html; the approval process usually only takes a few minutes but can take up to 72 hours. US citizens and US permanent residents do not require eTAs.
- Nationals of around 150 other countries must apply to the Canadian visa office in their home country for a temporary resident visa (TRV). See www.cic.gc.ca for full details.

Dos & Don'ts

- **Greetings** You will usually be greeted in stores and restaurants in French. It is fine to break into English, but learning basic French greetings is greatly appreciated.
- **Queues** Montréalers, and Canadians, are notoriously polite, especially when it comes to waiting in line. Any attempt to 'jump the queue' will result in an outburst of tutting.
- **Shoes** A rule respected (and enforced) in Québec in winter is to remove your shoes and place them in the tray (plateau) provided in homes, some cafes and even the odd boutique hotel. Winter footwear is covered in grit, mud and salt, which will soil carpets and wooden floors.

Responsible Travel

Overtourism

- Swap the region's blockbuster festivals for the huge array of lesser-known events that pop up here throughout the year. Movie fan? There's an excellent selection of film festivals to consider, especially in Montréal, with themes including documentaries, animation, cult movies and Francophone films. Even if you're not a festival fan, avoiding the summer peak and coming in spring or fall is an excellent way to sidestep the crowds, with the bonus of lower accommodation rates and less-busy attractions.
- Can't avoid a summer visit? Get creative while you're here by planning days out at lesser-known smaller attractions and neighbourhoods where crowds rarely congregate (p21). And on sunny days, swap jam-packed city restaurants for leisurely park picnics.

Lighter Footprints

- A car is not essential here; you can explore much of Montréal and Québec City via their transit systems. Handy transit passes are available in both cities, and they're a great option for urban adventuring.
- Support locally owned and operated businesses. That means shopping for gifts at independent stores and buying food and produce at neighbourhood shops and markets.

Language

Canada is officially a bilingual country with the majority of the population speaking English as their first language. In Québec, however, the dominant language is French. The local tongue is essentially the same as what you'd hear in France, and you'll have no problems being understood if you use standard French phrases (provided in this chapter).

The sounds used in spoken French can almost all be found in English. If you read our pronunciation guides as if they were English, you'll be understood.

To enhance your trip with a phrasebook, visit shop.lonelyplanet.com.

Basics

Hello.
Bonjour. bon·zhoor

Goodbye.
Au revoir. o·rer·vwa

How are you?
Comment allez-vous? ko·mon ta·lay·voo

I'm fine, thanks.
Bien, merci. byun mair·see

Please.
S'il vous plaît. seel voo play

Thank you.
Merci. mair·see

Excuse me.
Excusez-moi. ek·skew·zay·mwa

Sorry.
Pardon. par·don

Yes./No.
Oui./Non. wee/non

I don't understand.
Je ne comprends pas. zher ner kom·pron pa

Do you speak English?
Parlez-vous anglais? par·lay·voo ong·glay

Eating & Drinking

..., please.
..., s'il vous plaît. ... seel voo play

A coffee	*un café*	un ka·fay
A table for two	*une table pour deux*	ewn ta·bler poor der
Two beers	*deux bières*	der bee·yair

I'm a vegetarian.
Je suis végétarien/végétarienne. (m/f) zher swee vay·zhay·ta·ryun/vay·zhay·ta·ryen

That was delicious!
C'était délicieux! say·tay day·lee·syer

The bill, please.
L'addition, s'il vous plaît. la·dee·syon seel voo play

Shopping

I'd like to buy ...
Je voudrais acheter ... zher voo·dray ash·tay ...

I'm just looking.
Je regarde. zher rer·gard

Can I look at it?
Est-ce que je peux le voir? — es·ker zher per ler vwar

How much is it?
C'est combien? — say kom·byun

It's too expensive.
C'est trop cher. — say tro shair

There's a mistake in the bill.
Il y a une erreur dans la note — eel ya ewn ay·rer don la not

Emergencies

Help!
Au secours! — o skoor

Leave me alone!
Fichez-moi la paix! — fee·shay·mwa la pay

I'm lost.
Je suis perdu/perdue. — zhe swee pair·dew (m/f)

I'm ill.
Je suis malade. — zher swee ma·lad

Call a doctor!
Appelez un médecin! — a·play un mayd·sun

Call the police.
Appelez la police. — a·play la pol·ees

Call a doctor!
Appelez un médecin! — a·play un mayd·sun

Time & Dates

What time is it?
Y'est quelle heure? — il ay kel er

It's (eight) o'clock.
Il est (huit) heures. — il ay (weet) er

Half past (10).
(Dix) heures et demie. — (deez) er ay day·mee

morning
matin — ma·tun

afternoon
après-midi — a·pray·mee·dee

evening
soir — swar

yesterday
hier — yair

today
aujourd'hui — o·zhoor·dwee

tomorrow
demain — der·mun

Transportation

I want to go to ...
Je voudrais aller à ... — zher voo·dray a·lay a ...

At what time does it leave/arrive?
À quelle heure est-ce qu'il part/arrive? — a kel er es kil par/a·reev

Does it stop at ...?
Est-ce qu'il s'arrête à ...? — es·kil sa·ret a ...

I want to get off here.
Je veux descendre ici. — zher ver day·son·drer ee·see

a ... ticket
un billet ... — un bee·yay ...

one-way
simple — sum·pler

return
aller et retour — a·lay ay rer·toor

Behind the Scenes

Send Us Your Feedback

We love to hear from travelers – your comments help make our books better. We read every word, and we guarantee that your feedback goes straight to the authors. Visit **lonelyplanet.com/contact** to submit your updates and suggestions.

Note: We may edit, reproduce and incorporate your comments in Lonely Planet products such as guidebooks, websites and digital products, so let us know if you are happy to have your name acknowledged. For a copy of our privacy policy visit **lonelyplanet.com/legal**.

Phillip's Thanks

Thank you to Ben Buckner and the DEs. *Muchas gracias a Lalo (José Eduardo García Sánchez).* Thank you to Felix, Nick Zhang and the other Montréalers who offered guidance; and to Manuelle González Goretti for advice on the Eastern Townships and the Village.

Steve's Thanks

Un très grand merci to Gabriel d'Anjou Drouin and Maxime Aubin; Vicky Drolet; Sylvie Senécal and Pierre Lachance; and Carolyne Cyr and Pierre-André Guichoud. As always, this is dedicated to my spouse, Michael Rothschild.

Acknowledgements

Cover photograph: Carré St-Louis (p77), Montréal, Richard Cavalleri/ Shutterstock ©

Back cover photograph: St-Viateur Bagel (p97), Montréal, Joanna K Drakos/Shutterstock ©

This Book

This 2nd edition of Lonely Planet's *Pocket Montréal & Québec City* guidebook was curated by Regis St Louis and researched and written by John Lee, Steve Fallon and Phillip Tang.

This guidebook was produced by the following:

Destination Editor
Ben Buckner

Senior Product Editors
Angela Tinson, Grace Dobell, Martine Power, Saralinda Turner

Cartographers
Anthony Phelan, Corey Hutchison

Product Editors Amy Lysen, Kate McNamara, Ronan Abayawickrema

Book Designer
Virginia Moreno

Assisting Editors
Judith Bamber, Michelle Bennett, Victoria Harrison, Jodie Martire, Charlotte Orr, Maja Vatrić

Cover Researcher
Hannah Blackie

Thanks to Fergal Condon, Sonia Kapoor, Sandie Kestell, Kate Mathews, Genna Patterson, Kirsten Rawlings, Claire Rourke

Index

See also separate subindexes for:
Eating p158
Drinking p159
Entertainment p159
Shopping p159

Sights 000
Map Pages **000**

Sights 000
Map Pages **000**

Eating